A Guide to
Writing Research Papers

A Guide to
Writing Research Papers

Dorothea M. Berry
Reference Librarian
University of California, Riverside

Gordon P. Martin
College Librarian
Sacramento State College

McGraw-Hill Book Company

New York   St. Louis   San Francisco   Düsseldorf   Johannesburg
Kuala Lumpur   London   Mexico   Montreal   New Delhi
Panama   Rio de Janeiro   Singapore   Sydney   Toronto

A Guide to
Writing Research Papers

Library of Congress Catalog Card Number 70–139549

07–005031–7

1 2 3 4 5 6 7 8 9 0   B A B A   7 9 8 7 6 5 4 3 2 1

This book was set in Modern Number 21 by Monotype
Composition Company, Inc., and printed on permanent
paper and bound by George Banta Company, Inc. The
designer was Marsha Cohen; the drawings were done by
John Cordes, J. & R. Technical Services, Inc. The editors
were Robert Fry and David Dunham. Sally Ellyson
supervised production.

Preface

This manual has resulted from the authors' encounters with the problems and questions of undergraduate students writing term papers, of graduate students writing theses and dissertations, of faculty members preparing manuscripts for publication, and of their typists.

Although there are several guides to research paper writing on the market, the authors have become aware of the need for a guide that provides answers to questions concerning form more clearly and more concisely. It has been our purpose to produce a manual that presents the needed information in such a manner as to save the writers of papers time, frustration, and error.

Included are sections on the organization of the paper, documentation, presentation of tables and illustrations, and typing the manuscript. A separate section is devoted to instructions for the preparation of theses and dissertations. An appendix on research methods and sources includes sections on outlining and note-taking and lists of reference tools in the major academic subject fields.

Documentation in the humanities and social sciences fields is treated in one section, and the special forms for papers in the biological and physical sciences in a separate section. Each major scientific field is treated individually because of the variations in practice among these fields. This separate treatment results in more explicit and clearer information than the general statements with only a few examples which are given in some manuals.

A Guide to Writing Research Papers is a thorough revision and expansion of earlier editions issued in mimeographed form by the Bookstore of the University of California, Riverside, in 1956 and 1959. We are grateful to all who have given suggestions and criticisms. We wish especially to thank Mrs. Nanelia Doughty of the English faculty of the University of Nevada, Las Vegas, and Dr. Robert C. Neuman, Jr., Associate Professor of Chemistry and Graduate Advisor, University of California, Riverside, for their valuable suggestions for corrections and improvements in the manuscript. We wish to express our appreciation to Robert A. Fry, English Editor of the College Division of McGraw-Hill Book Company, his staff, and his reviewers for their interest and for their valuable criticism and suggestions. Their standards of quality are responsible for a more useful manual than this would otherwise have been.

We are grateful to Mrs. Marilyn Fisher and Mrs. Janet Warner for typing preliminary drafts of the manuscript and to Mrs. Cecilia Bernard for typing the final revision. We are also indebted to the UCR students who permitted us to use pages and illustrations from their papers and dissertations as examples, especially to Mrs. Sally Seekins for allowing us to use a research paper in its entirety.

Dorothea M. Berry
Gordon P. Martin

Contents

A Guide to
Writing Research Papers

I
Organization and Writing of the Paper

A. PARTS

Parts that may be included in a research paper are:

1. Title page
2. Outline
3. Table of contents
4. List of tables
5. List of illustrations
6. Text
7. Bibliography
8. Appendix

A short paper may consist only of a title page and the text. A longer paper may include, in addition, some of the parts listed above. For parts of a thesis or dissertation, see pages 27–28.

A sample research paper, complete with title page, outlines, text, and bibliography, appears on pages 13–26.

1. Title page

Every research paper should have a title page. The three parts are the title, the author's name, and the course number and date.

a. Title

The title of the paper, in capital letters, should be centered in the top third of the page. If it is longer than one line, it should be double-spaced and indented in inverted pyramid form.

b. Writer's name

The writer's name, with the word *by* two spaces above, should be centered on the page.

c. Course number and date

The course number on one line, and the date on a separate line two spaces below, should be centered in the lower third of the page.

If the writer wishes to include the instructor's name, it should be placed between the course number and the date with double-spacing separating the three items.

See page 13 for a sample title page of a research paper.

2. *Outline*

If an outline is required, it should follow the title page. It is numbered at the bottom of the page or pages with lowercase roman numerals beginning with page ii. The title page is counted as page i but the numeral is not typed on it. If an outline is not required as a part of the finished paper, the student should make one for his own use before he begins to write the paper. The purpose and types of outlines are discussed on page 152. Sample outlines are given on pages 14–15.

3. *Table of contents*

A paper long enough to be divided into chapters or sections should have a table of contents. If an outline is required as a part of the paper, it takes the place of a table of contents. If an outline is not required, a table of contents should be included and numbered as page ii.

Detailed instructions for preparing the table of contents are given on pages 29, 34. Various styles are illustrated on pages 35–37.

4–5. *List of tables and list of illustrations*

If there are several tables or illustrations in the text, there should be a list in the preliminary pages. The list of tables follows the table of contents. The list of illustrations follows the list of tables. These pages are numbered with lowercase roman numerals at the bottom of the pages.

Detailed instructions are given on page 38 for a list of tables, and on page 38 for a list of illustrations. A sample list of tables is given on page 39, and sample lists of illustrations on pages 40–42.

6. *Text*

A short paper may have few or no divisions. The text may begin with an introductory statement or paragraph and close with a summary statement or conclusion. A longer paper should be divided into chapters or sections, the first of which may be an introduction, and the last a summary or conclusions.

The discussion of divisions of the text and the use of headings, given in the section on theses and dissertations, pages 38, 43, applies to any long, formal research paper.

7. *Bibliography*

A bibliography should be given for a research paper unless the paper is short and adequate documentation is given in footnotes.

A discussion of the bibliography, including its arrangement and form, and examples of entries for various types of publications, are given on pages 74–88.

A sample bibliography for a research paper is given on pages 25–26.

8. *Appendix*

Only a long, formal research paper would include an appendix. See page 44 for description and instructions.

B. FOOTNOTES

Footnotes should be used in a research paper to acknowledge quotations, statements, or ideas taken from another author and to substantiate facts or statements by citing the source of information. Footnotes may also be used for explanatory comments. A detailed discussion of footnotes and examples of form for various types of publications are given on pages 48–74. See also pages 17–24 for footnotes in the sample research paper.

C. ENUMERATION

Numbers or letters used in enumerating items in the text should be enclosed in parentheses.

He criticizes the conservative point of view on four points: (1) examinations and certificates, (2) concern with an educational elite, (3) compatibility of the traditional and the new activities, (4) alleged replacement of an adult education movement by an educational service.

If each item in a series begins a new line, parentheses are omitted and arabic numerals followed by periods are used, listed one directly under the one above.

1. Institutions originally developed for another educational purpose
2. Agencies originally developed for noneducational purposes
3. Agencies originally established to serve both young people and adults
4. Agencies initially established entirely for adult education

When items are in outline form with subdivisions, the following scheme of enumeration and indention is used:

```
I.   The Role of Institutions of Higher Education
     A.  United States
         1.  Universities
             a.  State
             b.  Private
         2.  Colleges
             a.  Four-year Liberal Arts Colleges
                 (1)  Public
                 (2)  Private
             b.  Junior Colleges
                 (1)  Public
                 (2)  Private
```

    B.   Canada
        1. Universities
        2. Colleges
II. The Role of Other Agencies
    A. Public Schools
    B. Libraries
    C. Business, Industry, and Labor
    D. Specialized Agencies

D. QUOTATIONS

1. Use

Quotations used must be acknowledged by means of footnotes. Footnoting is explained in detail on pages 48–74.

If the writer wishes to quote extensively from a copyrighted work, he must obtain permission from the owner of the copyright. Permission from the author is necessary to quote from unpublished material.

Direct quotations should correspond exactly with the original in wording, spelling, and punctuation. Exceptions are discussed in sections 4–8 below.

2. Prose

Short prose quotations should be run into the text of the paper and enclosed in double quotation marks.

> In an address at the University of North Carolina, October 12, 1961, President Kennedy remarked: "Peace and freedom do not come cheap, and we are destined . . . to live out most if not all of our lives in uncertainty and challenge and peril."

A prose quotation longer than four or five typewritten lines, or more than one sentence, should be set off from the text by three spaces and indented in block form five spaces from the left margin. It should be single-spaced with no quotation marks at beginning or end.

> In his "divided house" speech at the Republican State Convention in Springfield, Illinois, June 16, 1858, Abraham Lincoln made these statements on the slavery issue:

> > We are now far into the fifth year since a policy was initiated with the avowed object and confident promise of putting an end to slavery agitation. Under the operation of that policy, that agitation has not only not ceased but has constantly augmented. In my opinion, it will not cease until a crisis shall have been reached and passed. "A house divided against itself cannot stand." I believe this government cannot endure permanently half slave and half free. I do not expect the Union to be dissolved—I do not expect the house to fall—but I do expect it will cease to be divided. It will become all one thing, or all the other.

Shorter prose quotations may be set off from the text for the purpose of emphasis.

3. Poetry

Poetry of more than two lines in length should be set off from the text, single-spaced, and centered on the page with no quotation marks at the beginning or end. The length and indention of the lines in the original should be followed.

```
    Emily Dickinson's compactness of expression is illustrated
by this quatrain:

            Who has not found the heaven below
                Will fail of it above.
            God's residence is next to mine,
                His furniture is love.
```

If two lines of poetry are run into the text, they are enclosed in quotation marks and the division of the lines is indicated by a diagonal line.

```
    As Thomas Gray noted, "Full many a flow'r is born to blush
unseen / And waste its sweetness on the desert air."
```

4. Quotation marks

Quotations run into the text require double quotation marks at the beginning and end, and any internal double quotation marks in the material quoted must be changed to single quotation marks.

```
    Referring to her blindness, Helen Keller said, "It gives me
a deep comforting sense that 'things seen are temporal and
things unseen are eternal.'"
```

Double quotation marks within the material quoted are retained in single-spaced, indented quotations. See the second example in the section on prose quotations, page 4.

Quotations displayed at the heads of chapters or other major sections are not enclosed in quotation marks. The quotation is placed three spaces below the chapter title, single-spaced, and indented in paragraph form. The source, preceded by a dash and aligned with the right margin, is given immediately below a quotation used for this purpose.

```
                            CHAPTER I


                            CURIOSITAS


    I have often said that man's unhappiness arises from one
thing only, namely that he cannot abide quietly in one room.
                                    —Pascal, Pensées
```

Three spaces are allowed between the quotation and the first line of text.

5. *Capitalization of the first word of a quotation*

The capitalization of the first word of a quotation may be changed in the following cases.

If a quotation is incorporated into the writer's sentence, the first word of the quotation is not capitalized although it is capitalized in the original.

```
    Kipling warned that "the female of the species is more
deadly than the male."
```

A lowercase letter may be changed to a capital if it is preceded by a colon or terminal punctuation in the text immediately before the quotation.

```
    "To steer clear of permanent alliances, with any portion of
the foreign world" was Washington's advice.
```

A lowercase letter may be changed to a capital if the quotation forms a complete sentence although it was not a complete sentence in the original.

```
    "Give me liberty or give me death."
```

6. *Omissions*

Words, phrases, sentences, or lines may be omitted from quotations. The omissions are indicated by spaced periods. Three spaced periods should be used to indicate an omission within a sentence. See the first example in the section on prose quotations, page 4. If an omission follows a complete sentence, three spaced periods are used in addition to the period or other terminal punctuation.

```
    In an address in Independence Hall, Philadelphia, on
February 22, 1861, Lincoln said:  "Now in my view of the present
aspect of affairs, there is no need of bloodshed and war. . . .
The government will not use force, unless force is used against
it."
```

A single line of spaced periods is used to indicate omission of one or more lines of a poem. A line of spaced periods may also be used to indicate omission of a paragraph or more of prose, but it is preferable to use separate quotations if the omissions are long.

7. *Interpolations*

Interpolations into a quotation may be made for the purpose of clarifying the meaning, supplying missing words, or making corrections. Interpolations must be enclosed in square brackets.

```
    "In my opinion, it [slavery agitation] will not cease until
a crisis has been reached."
```

The Latin word *sic*, meaning "thus" or "so," may be inserted in brackets after words that are misspelled or incorrectly used to indicate that the error is in the original material.

"Some species of wild life are in danger of exstinction
[sic] due to environmental pollution."

8. *Italics*

If the writer wishes to emphasize words in a quotation, he may underline them to indicate italics. This must be explained by the notation [italics mine] enclosed in square brackets immediately following the underlined portion, or by a parenthetical note (italics mine) following the quotation, or in a footnote.

In his Inaugural Address, January 20, 1961, John F. Kennedy
said: "We observe today not a victory of party but a <u>celebra-
tion of freedom</u> [italics mine] symbolizing an end as well as a
beginning, signifying renewal as well as change."

or

"We observe today not a victory of party but a <u>celebration
of freedom</u> symbolizing an end as well as a beginning, signifying
renewal as well as change." (Italics mine.)

E. STYLE

In the course of writing a paper, the student may encounter problems of sentence structure, grammar, word usage, spelling, word division, punctuation, capitalization, and the use of numbers. Dictionaries supply the answers to many questions. There are also several excellent handbooks which the student will find helpful in these matters of style.

1. *Dictionaries*

Dictionaries are useful for:

correct spelling
hyphenation of compound words
syllabification (for division of words at the end of lines)
correct usage through indication of parts of speech and definitions
choice of words through listing of synonyms with differentiation of meanings, and listing
   of antonyms

a. Unabridged dictionaries

The standard unabridged dictionaries are:

Webster's New International Dictionary of the English Language. 2d ed. Springfield, Mass.:
   G. & C. Merriam Company, 1960.
      A revision of the second edition published in 1934. Includes 600,000 entries.
      Gives etymologies, illustrative quotations, synonyms, and antonyms. Foreign
      phrases, abbreviations, proverbs, names of fiction, and proper names are in the
      main vocabulary. All vocabulary entries with definitions are in the upper section
      of the page. Cross references, obsolete words, foreign language quotations and

proverbs are in the lower section of the page. Abbreviations, signs and symbols, a biographical dictionary, a gazetteer, an addenda of new words, and spelling rules appear in separate sections.

Webster's Third New International Dictionary of the English Language. Springfield, Mass.: G. & C. Merriam Company, 1961.

A completely new work presenting the language as it is currently used. Defines 450,000 terms. Gives etymologies and synonyms. Illustrations are mostly from mid-twentieth century sources. Abbreviations and foreign phrases are included in the main vocabulary. Includes special sections on spelling, plurals, capitalization, italicization, compounds, and punctuation.

Funk & Wagnalls New Standard Dictionary of the English Language. New York: Funk & Wagnalls Company, 1963.

First published in 1913. Includes 450,000 terms. Gives etymologies, illustrative phrases and quotations, synonyms, and antonyms. Abbreviations, frequently used foreign words and phrases, and proper names such as biographical, geographical, mythological, fictional, and biblical are in the main alphabet. Separate sections include new words and additional meanings, foreign words and phrases, and compound words.

Somewhat less comprehensive than the dictionaries listed above is:

The Random House Dictionary of the English Language. New York: Random House, 1966.

Defines 260,000 terms. Useful features include illustrative examples after definitions, synonym and antonym lists, usage notes, and etymologies. Personal and place names and foreign words and phrases are included in the main listing. Separate sections include signs and symbols, a basic manual of style, and a gazetteer.

b. Desk dictionaries

Desk dictionaries are adequate for many purposes. Those listed below are recommended as authoritative and up-to-date.

American College Dictionary. New York: Random House, 1967.

Contains 132,000 entries in one alphabetical list, including names of persons and places, abbreviations, and foreign words and phrases. Includes etymologies and synonyms. A guide to usage is given in an appendix.

American Heritage Dictionary of the English Language. Boston: American Heritage Publishing Co. and Houghton Mifflin Company, 1969.

A new work containing 155,000 entries. Personal and place names, foreign words and phrases, slang, cross references, and abbreviations are included in the main listing. Entries include, in addition to definitions, variant spellings, illustrations of usage, synonyms, and etymologies. Illustrated with line drawings and photographs. Introductory essays on the history and origin of the language, usage, dialects, grammar and meaning, spelling and pronunciation, and computers in language analysis and lexicography.

Cassell's English Dictionary. Rev. and enl. by Arthur L. Hayward and John J. Sparkes. London: Cassell, 1962.

> Includes 130,000 words and phrases current among English-speaking peoples of the world, with many technical and scientific terms in common use. Proper names are included in the main listing. Separate sections for pronunciation of proper names; foreign words and phrases; and abbreviations, signs, and symbols.

Funk & Wagnalls Standard College Dictionary. New York: Funk & Wagnalls Company, 1963.

> Includes 150,000 terms. Personal names, geographical names, foreign words and phrases, and abbreviations are in the main listing. Definitions are followed by examples of usage, synonyms, and etymologies. Includes a reference guide to punctuation, capitalization, correspondence, manuscript preparation, and proofreaders' marks.

Webster's New World Dictionary of the American Language. College ed. Cleveland: World Publishing Company, 1964.

> First published in 1953. A new work containing 142,000 entries in one listing, including proper names, abbreviations, foreign words and phrases, colloquialisms, and slang. Includes etymologies, synonyms, and illustrative examples of usage.

Webster's Seventh New Collegiate Dictionary. Springfield, Mass.: G. & C. Merriam Company, 1963.

> Based on *Webster's Third New International Dictionary.* Contains 130,000 entries. Includes etymologies and synonyms. Appendixes include abbreviations, a biographical section, a gazetteer, and a section on spelling.

It may be desirable to consult dictionaries for the specific subject areas concerned. The appendix, pages 140–152, lists dictionaries in areas such as art, music, psychology, religion, anthropology, sociology, political science, economics, education, law, medicine, chemistry, physics, geology, and biology. These special subject dictionaries can be located through the card catalog by looking under the subject and the subheading "Dictionaries" (e.g. Art-Dictionaries).

2. Handbooks

The handbooks listed in this section are for the humanities and social sciences fields. Students writing papers in the biological sciences, chemistry, geology, physics, and psychology should consult style manuals for these particular fields. These manuals are listed and described in Section VI, Scientific Papers, pages 107–116.

a. Handbooks covering several aspects of style

Baker, Sheridan. *The Complete Stylist.* New York: Thomas Y. Crowell Company, 1966.

> Sections on the basic structure of the paper, outlines, paragraphs, sentences, punctuation, words, types of essays, and writing the research paper (choice of a subject, use of the library, documentation). Appendixes include A Writer's Grammar, A Glossary of Usage, Rhetorical Devices, and a specimen research paper.

Chicago. University. Press. *A Manual of Style.* 12th ed. rev. Chicago: University of Chicago Press, 1969.
> Part 2, Style, includes sections on punctuation, spelling and distinctive treatment of words, names and terms, numbers, foreign languages in type, quotations, illustrations, captions, legends, tables, mathematics in type, abbreviations, notes and footnotes, bibliographies, public documents, and indexes.

Hook, Julius N. *Hook's Guide to Good Writing.* New York: Ronald Press, 1962.
> Approximately 1650 entries or articles arranged alphabetically, giving answers to questions about grammar, good writing style, usage, and mechanical features of writing including punctuation and spelling.

Lambuth, David, and others. *The Golden Book on Writing.* New York: Viking Press, 1964.
> Concise treatment of organization, the paragraph, the sentence, choice of words, letter writing, punctuation, style, and business writing.

Perrin, Porter G., and George H. Smith. *The Perrin-Smith Handbook of Current English.* 2d ed. Chicago: Scott, Foresman and Company, 1962.
> Major sections on grammar, punctuation, effectiveness, and composition.

Strunk, William, Jr. *The Elements of Style.* New York: Macmillan Company, 1959.
> Short sections on elementary rules of usage, elementary principles of composition, matters of form, words and expressions commonly misused, and style.

United States Government Printing Office. *Style Manual.* Rev. ed. Washington, D.C.: Government Printing Office, 1967.
> Rules for preparation of copy for the Government Printing Office, including capitalization, spelling, compound words, punctuation, abbreviations, numerals, italics, signs and symbols.

b. Handbooks on particular aspects of style

(1) Word usage

Bernstein, Theodore M. *The Careful Writer: A Modern Guide to English Usage.* New York: Atheneum, 1965.
> Words and phrases arranged alphabetically, with explanations and examples of correct usage.

Bryant, Margaret M. *Current American Usage.* New York: Funk & Wagnalls Company, 1962.
> Information about frequently debated points of usage. Includes citations to dictionaries, treatises of linguists, periodical articles, and special investigations undertaken for this book.

Evans, Bergen, and Cornelia Evans. *Dictionary of Contemporary American Usage.* New York: Random House, 1957.
> Alphabetically arranged entries explaining word usage, grammar, figures of speech, phrases, and idioms.

Follett, Wilson. *Modern American Usage.* New York: Hill & Wang, 1966.
> Alphabetically arranged entries cover problems of diction, idiom, syntax, usage, and style. Includes an appendix on the use of *shall* and *will* and an appendix on punctuation.

Fowler, Henry W. *A Dictionary of Modern English Usage.* 2d ed. rev. by Sir Ernest Gowers. Oxford: At the Clarendon Press, 1965.
> A modernization of the original edition published in 1926. Contains short articles on word usage, indicating the correct usage by examples.

(2) Synonyms

Hayakawa, Samuel I. *Funk & Wagnalls Modern Guide to Synonyms and Related Words.* New York: Funk & Wagnalls Company, 1968.
> Alphabetically arranged. Synonyms with distinctions in meanings, cross references, and antonyms.

March, Francis A., and Francis A. March, Jr. *March's Thesaurus and Dictionary of the English Language.* New Supplement by R. A. Goodwin. Garden City, N.Y.: Doubleday & Company, 1968.
> Words arranged alphabetically. Definitions given for each word with distinctions between related and synonymous words. Includes cross references to other terms. Supplement includes words and phrases that have come into use since 1900.

Roget's International Thesaurus. 3d ed. New York: Thomas Y. Crowell Company, 1962.
> Words grouped according to ideas, with an alphabetical index. Synonyms are grouped under main entries according to parts of speech (nouns, verbs, adjectives, adverbs)

Webster's New Dictionary of Synonyms. Springfield, Mass.: G. & C. Merriam Company, 1968.
> A dictionary of discriminated synonyms with antonyms and analagous and contrasted words.

(3) Grammar

Curme, George O. *Principles and Practice of English Grammar.* New York: Barnes & Noble, 1947.
> Major sections on parts of speech, inflection, syntax of the sentence, and syntax of the parts of speech.

Fernald, James C. *English Grammar Simplified.* Rev. ed. New York: Funk & Wagnalls Company, 1963.
> Sections on parts of speech, the sentence, punctuation, and the mechanics of writing.

Hook, Julius N., and E. G. Mathews. *Modern American Grammar and Usage.* New York: Ronald Press Company, 1956.
> A guide to sentence structure and parts of speech.

House, Homer, and Susan E. Harman. *Descriptive English Grammar*. 2d ed. rev. by Susan E. Harman. Englewood Cliffs, N.J.: Prentice-Hall, 1950.
> Part One, Grammatical Form, is organized in chapters on parts of speech. Part Two, Sentence Analysis, deals with the elements of the sentence, simple and complex sentences.

Pence, Raymond W., and D. W. Emery. *A Grammar of Present-Day English*. 2d ed. New York: Macmillan Company, 1963.
> Part One, Syntax; Part Two, Form and Usages (parts of speech). Includes an appendix, The Diagram in Grammatical Analysis.

(4) Punctuation

Partridge, Eric. *You Have a Point There: A Guide to Punctuation and Its Allies*. With a Chapter on American Practice by John W. Clark. London: Hamish Hamilton, 1953.
> Deals with the theory and practice of punctuation. Book I, Punctuation, contains chapters on individual punctuation marks. Book II, Allies and Accessories, contains chapters on capitals, italics, quotation marks, hyphens, obliques, braces, apostrophes, indentions, and paragraphing. Book III, Orchestration, deals with punctuation in relation to quoted matter, and gives examples of punctuation in paragraphs. Book IV deals with differences between American and British practice.

Shaw, Harry. *Punctuate It Right!* New York: Barnes & Noble, 1963.
> Part One, What Punctuation Is and Does, includes chapters on punctuation for clarity, a brief survey of punctuation, trends in modern American punctuation, and the primary purposes of punctuation and mechanics. Part Two, Individual Marks, is arranged alphabetically by the names of the marks of punctuation with subdivisions under each. Includes numerous examples.

Summey, George, Jr. *American Punctuation*. New York: Ronald Press Company, 1949.
> Chapters 1–8 deal with structural punctuation, paragraph breaks, and marks used within and between sentences. Chapters 9–11 deal with quotation marks, hyphens, apostrophes, and abbreviation periods.

SAMPLE RESEARCH PAPER

With Sample Topic and Sentence Outlines

THE EDUCATIONAL DIFFICULTIES OF CULTURALLY DIFFERENT STUDENTS

AND WHAT CAN BE DONE ABOUT THEM

by

Sarah F. Seekins

Education 201D

January 16, 1967

THE EDUCATIONAL DIFFICULTIES OF CULTURALLY DIFFERENT STUDENTS

AND WHAT CAN BE DONE ABOUT THEM

TOPIC OUTLINE

I. Definition of culturally different students

II. Problems of culturally different students

   A. Lack of knowledge of classroom behavior

   B. Lack of speed in problem solving

   C. Anti-intellectual attitude

   D. Expectation of failure

III. Changes needed in educational methods and motives

   A. More respect for students

   B. Re-examination of school rewards

   C. Meaningful learning situations

   D. Programmed learning

IV. Conclusion

THE EDUCATIONAL DIFFICULTIES OF CULTURALLY DIFFERENT STUDENTS

AND WHAT CAN BE DONE ABOUT THEM

SENTENCE OUTLINE

I.   Culturally different students are students who do not hold the same cultural values as the vast majority of teachers and schools.

II. The culturally different student has special problems that affect school achievement.

    A. He lacks knowledge of what is expected of him in the classroom.

    B. His slowness in problem solving is misinterpreted by teachers as poor mental processes.

    C. He is even more anti-intellectual than the national norm.

    D. Teachers and the student himself expect failure of him.

III. To reverse the trend of increase in numbers of the culturally different, major changes in educational methods and motives are necessary.

    A. Teachers must respect these students.

    B. Teachers must re-examine rewards for educational achievement.

    C.   Teachers must provide meaningful learning situations.

    D.   Programmed learning and teaching machines are effective with culturally different students.

IV. It is concluded that there is little hope for the culturally different students unless new methods and attitudes are adopted and tested.

THE EDUCATIONAL DIFFICULTIES OF CULTURALLY DIFFERENT STUDENTS

AND WHAT CAN BE DONE ABOUT THEM

By culturally different students, I am referring to the many different groups of students who do not hold the same cultural values as the vast majority of teachers and the schools they teach in. The culturally different are in large measure the culturally deprived—people of the lower and working classes. Children from this economic background are part of the culture of poverty in which attitudes and motivations differ tremendously from the middle class values of the American educational establishment.[1] Also under the heading of culturally different should be included the small group of those students from comfortable and prosperous backgrounds who at present are not succeeding in school because they cannot or refuse to accept the values of today's schools.[2] From a very short teaching experience, I think these students can profit greatly by the same sort of program designed to reach their much less fortunate classmates.

The primary problem facing the culturally different child is his lack of knowledge concerning what is expected of him in

---

[1]Hyman Rodman, "On Understanding Lower-Class Behavior," Social and Economic Studies, VIII (December, 1959), 442.

[2]Willard J. Congreve, "Not All the Disadvantaged Are Poor," PTA Magazine, LX (February, 1966), 15.

2

the classroom. He usually comes from a background where
discipline is rather strict and physical punishment is the
reward for misbehavior.[3] Often such children are put into a
progressive kindergarten, a situation of minimum restraints.
The child soon oversteps the bounds assumed by the middle class
teacher since these children do not hold the middle class values
that such things as acting out aggression are bad. Culturally
different students need direction and control. They cannot
handle too much classroom freedom.[4] This is simply because of
the ignorance of acceptable classroom behavior.[5]

Culturally different students are typically described as
"slow" students, with "slow" synonymous with "poor". Such a
student, when given an academic problem, needs more time to
arrive at an answer and to generalize from the answer. The
student, because he lacks facility with words, approaches problems in a physical manner. He must "do as much as he can in
thinking through a problem."[6] This style of thinking takes more

---

[3]S. M. Miller and Frank Riessman, "The Working Class Sub-
culture: A New View," Social Problems, IX (Summer, 1961), 93.

[4]Daniel U. Levine, "Differentiating Instruction for Disadvantaged Students," The Educational Forum, XXX (January,
1966), 144.

[5]Shelly P. Koenigsberg, "Teaching Disadvantaged Youth in
Secondary School," Journal of Secondary Education, XLI (January,
1966), 20.

[6]Frank Riessman, The Culturally Deprived Child (New York:
Harper and Row, 1962), p. 66.

3

time than the verbal approach to problem solving. Riessman

suggests that this method does not connote retardation but is

part of a pattern found in one type of highly creative person.[7]

All too often the lack of speed evidenced by the culturally

different is interpreted by teachers as indicating poor mental

processes rather than simply another style of thinking.[8]

American culture has not been noted for its devotion to

scholarship and intellectualism,[9] and the culturally different

tend to be even more anti-intellectual than is the national

norm.

> He is pragmatic and anti-intellectual. It is the end
> result that counts. What can be seen and felt is more
> likely to be real and true in his perspective. His
> practical orientation does not encourage abstract ideas.
> Education, for what it does for one in terms of oppor-
> tunities, may be desirable, but abstract, intellectual
> speculation, ideas not rooted in the realities of the
> present, are not useful, and indeed may be harmful.[10]

The culturally different male, especially, places much

value on ruggedness, physical strength, and practicality. The

school, for such boys, is much too prissy. The school demands

behavior which is not masculine in the boys' eyes. They must

---

[7]*Ibid.*, p. 73.

[8]Riessman, *op. cit.*, p. 64.

[9]Richard Hofstadter, <u>Anti-Intellectualism in American Life</u>
(New York: Random House, 1962), p. 6.

[10]Riessman, *op. cit.*, p. 28.

4

restrict their physical activity. They must be neat. They

must be quiet and obedient. Intellectual activity is not seen

by them as a masculine activity.[11]

The culturally different student is slow in learning, often

a discipline problem, and unmotivated to learn what the teacher

wants to teach. The overwhelming tendency is for the teacher to

respond as if the child were a poor student. The child fed

upon school failure and defeat soon adopts the school's evalua-

tion of his worthiness as his own. Very early in the game the

culturally different student sees himself as a failure.[12] This

perhaps is the greatest handicap of all. Teachers and the

student himself expect so little achievement and so much failure

of him that it seems almost impossible to all concerned that the

student could get anything out of school at all.[13]

The enormity of the problem becomes instantly apparent when

it is realized that the culturally different make up one third

of our big city school enrollment. By 1970, the figure is

expected to be one half.[14] In order to reverse this trend,

---

[11]*Ibid*., p. 34.

[12]E. C. Harrison, "Working at Improving the Motivational
and Achievement Levels of the Deprived," Journal of Negro
Education, XXXII (Summer, 1963), 302.

[13]Allan C. Ornstein, "Effective Schools for 'Disadvantaged'
Children," Journal of Secondary Education, XL (March, 1965),
106.

[14]Riessman, *op. cit*., p. 1.

5

major overhauls of our educational methods and motives must come about.

First of all, our well-meaning teachers must give up loving their students and, instead, honestly respect them.[15] Culturally different students do not need to be loved and pitied as much as respected as worthwhile human beings. Teachers must come to these children with knowledge of how they think and how they learn. As of yet, too "little attention has been given to a view of the behavior and conditions of socially disadvantaged children as given information which the school might use in the design of meaningful and appropriate learning experiences."[16] Until teachers respect students as they are at present, with their abilities and disabilities, the low esteem of culturally different students will not be raised.

Another element of the educational process teachers must re-examine is the rewards that are promised to students for more or less successfully putting up with and getting through the system. The most common one is "a diploma is the key to a good job." For most culturally different students a job is too far in the future for them to put up with the frustrations of the

---

[15]Arthur Pearl, "As a Psychologist Sees Pressures on Disadvantaged Teen-Agers," NEA Journal, LIV (February, 1965), 19.

[16]Edmund W. Gordon, "Characteristics of Socially Disadvantaged Children," Review of Educational Research, XXXV (December, 1965), 384.

6

present in the school.[17] For those that can see that far ahead,

in our era of technology, the alternatives seem to be become an

unemployed high-school dropout or become an unemployed high-

school graduate.[18] Clearly, career advancement motivations for

academic achievement are not enough. The school must give cul-

turally different children a taste of success now and not hold

it back until graduation. Ausebel suggests that the best ap-

proach may be for teachers to, for the moment, forget these

students are unmotivated to learn. Given a chance at learning,

the students may surprise everyone by doing just that. Thus

motivation can be "developed retroactively from successful

educational achievement."[19]

When working with the culturally different students,

teachers must take into account under what conditions these

students learn best. For these students "meaningless learning

cannot generate interest and attention."[20] They literally can-

not sit still for rote learning. The most meaningful learning

for them comes from "concrete experiences in which the indi-

---

[17]David P. Ausebel, "Teaching Strategy for Culturally
Deprived Pupils: Cognitive and Motivational Considerations,"
School Review, LXXI (Winter, 1965), 459-460.

[18]Pearl, loc. cit.

[19]Ausebel, op. cit., p. 461.

[20]Koenigsberg, loc. cit.

7

vidual is physically involved. ..."[21] "Acting out" lessons is

very helpful. Since culturally different students have a

limited background of experiences, examples must be drawn from

everyday occurrences from which they can be led on to more ab-

stract ideas.[22] Not all the culturally different are alike, so

teaching must be tailored as much as possible to individual

students' needs. Further, the teacher must be sure that the

student realizes he has been learning even more than he is aware

of. This sounds much like what everyone would call "good

teaching" and that is certainly what these students need. It

also sounds like programmed learning, and that is perhaps the

key to the break-through the schools need to reach these

students.

Given the high student-teacher ratio alone, the need for

programmed learning and teaching machines becomes apparent.[23]

Some criticize the brevity of teaching machine forms as not

being conducive to seeing the development of concepts and logi-

cal relationships, but many see programmed learning as one of

the best strategies for dealing with culturally different stu-

---

[21]Catherine Brunner, "Deprivation--Its Effects, Its Remedies," Educational Leadership, XXIII (November, 1965), 104.

[22]Koenigsberg, op. cit., p. 18.

[23]Martin Deutsch, "Some Psychosocial Aspects of Learning in
the Disadvantaged," Teachers College Record, LXVII (January,
1966), 263.

8

dents.[24] Programmed instruction is appealing to these students
for several reasons. More than any other method it gives an
instant reward and feeling of accomplishment. It allows the
students to progress at their own speed for all different subjects. It is attractive because it appeals to their sense of
excitement at "new gadgets."[25] In one small study involving
some ninth grade potential dropouts in Paterson, New Jersey, the
use of teaching machines provided for more individualized instruction and brought about more student motivation and
participation.[26]

It would seem that programmed instruction would have
benefits for all students, not only the culturally different.
This is probably true. However, the school must at present be
most conscious of the needs of the children it is not reaching.
The others can adapt to new methods and succeed anyway. There
is little hope for the culturally different unless new methods
and attitudes are adopted and tested.

_____

[24]Ausebel, op. cit., p. 455.

[25]Riessman, op. cit., p. 28.

[26]Moe Liss, "Stem Dropout Tide—Here's How," The American
School Board Journal, CLIII (September, 1966), 44-45.

9

BIBLIOGRAPHY

Arnez, Nancy L. "The Effect of Teacher Attitudes Upon the
    Culturally Different." School and Society, XCIV (March 19,
    1966), 149–152.

Ausebel, David P. "The Effects of Cultural Deprivation on
    Learning Patterns." Audiovisual Instruction, X (January,
    1965), 10–12.

Ausebel, David P. "A Teaching Strategy for Culturally Deprived
    Pupils: Cognitive and Motivational Considerations." School
    Review, LXXI (Winter, 1963), 454–463.

Bettelheim, Bruno. "Teaching the Disadvantaged." NEA Journal,
    LIV (September, 1965), 8–12.

Brunner, Catherine. "Deprivation––Its Effects, Its Remedies."
    Educational Leadership, XXIII (November, 1965), 103–107.

Centers, Richard. The Psychology of Social Classes. Princeton,
    N.J.: Princeton University Press, 1949.

Congreve, Willard J. "Not All the Disadvantaged Are Poor." PTA
    Magazine, LX (February, 1966), 15–17.

Davis, Allison. Social–Class Influences Upon Learning. Cam-
    bridge, Mass.: Harvard University Press, 1952.

Deutsch, Martin. "Some Psychological Aspects of Learning in the
    Disadvantaged." Teachers College Record, LXVII (January,
    1966), 260–265.

Gordon, Edmund W. "Characteristics of Socially Disadvantaged
    Children." Review of Educational Research, XXXV (December,
    1965), 377–385.

Harrison, E. C. "Working at Improving the Motivational and
    Achievement Levels of the Deprived." Journal of Negro
    Education, XXXII (Summer, 1963), 301–307.

Hofstadter, Richard. Anti–Intellectualism in American Life.
    New York: Random House, 1962.

10

Hyman, Herbert H. "The Value Systems of Different Classes: A
    Social Psychological Contribution to the Analysis of Strati-
    fication." In <u>Class, Status and Power: A Reader in Social
    Stratification</u>, edited by Reinhard Bendix and S. M. Lipset.
    Glencoe, Ill.: Free Press, 1953. Pp. 426–442.

Koenigsberg, Shelly P. "Teaching Disadvantaged Youth in Sec-
    ondary School." <u>Journal of Secondary Education</u>, XLI
    (January, 1966), 17–24.

Levine, Daniel U. "Differentiating Instruction for Disad-
    vantaged Students." <u>The Educational Forum</u>, XXX (January,
    1966), 143–146.

Liss, Moe. "Stem Dropout Tide—Here's How," <u>The American School
    Board Journal</u>, CLIII (September, 1966), 44–45.

Miller, S. M., and Frank Riessman. "The Working Class Subcul-
    ture: A New View." <u>Social Problems</u>, IX (Summer, 1961),
    86–97.

Ornstein, Allan C. "Effective Schools for 'Disadvantaged'
    Children." <u>Journal of Secondary Education</u>, XL (March, 1965),
    105–109.

Pearl, Arthur. "As a Psychologist Sees Pressures on Disad-
    vantaged Teen-Agers." <u>NEA Journal</u>, LIV (February, 1965),
    18–19, 21.

Riessman, Frank. <u>The Culturally Deprived Child</u>. New York:
    Harper and Row, 1962.

Riessman, Frank. "The Overlooked Positives of Disadvantaged
    Groups." <u>Journal of Negro Education</u>, XXXIV (Spring, 1965),
    160–166.

Rodman, Hyman. "On Understanding Lower-Class Behavior." <u>Social
    and Economic Studies</u>, VIII (December, 1959), 441–449.

Siller, Jerome. "Socioeconomic Status and Conceptual Thinking."
    <u>The Journal of Abnormal and Social Psychology</u>, LV (November,
    1957), 365–371.

Warren, Paul B. "An Educational Approach for the Culturally
    Disadvantaged." <u>Journal of Negro Education</u>, XXXV (Summer,
    1963), 283–286.

II
Theses
and Dissertations

In this section, matters pertaining exclusively to theses and dissertations are discussed. The sections on research, documentation, tables and illustrations, scientific papers, and typing the manuscript apply to all types of research papers, including theses and dissertations.

A. COMMITTEE APPROVAL

A graduate student must have the approval of his thesis or doctoral committee for the subject and the plan of treatment of his thesis or dissertation. As his work progresses, he should consult with his committee to be certain he is meeting the requirements and standards of his department.

B. LOCAL REQUIREMENTS

Most institutions, through an agency such as the graduate office or archivist's office, issue special instructions concerning local requirements for the number of copies to be submitted, the date when copies are due in order for the degree to be granted at the end of a semester or quarter, how and where they are to be submitted, methods of reproduction acceptable, and some instructions on physical format. The student should acquire a copy of such instructions and follow them, since requirements vary in different institutions. Most institutions furnish the services of a thesis manuscript adviser to answer questions concerning details of form.

C. ARRANGEMENT OF THE PARTS

Normally a thesis or dissertation consists of three main parts: the preliminaries, the text, and the reference matter. The following sequence of parts should be observed, except for local variations.

1. Preliminaries

a. Title page
b. Copyright page (optional)
c. Approval page

d. Vita, publications, and fields of study (for dissertations)
e. Dedication page (optional)
f. Preface, including acknowledgments
g. Abstract
h. Table of contents
i. List of tables
j. List of illustrations

2. Text

a. Introduction
b. Main body, usually containing chapters or their equivalent
c. Conclusions

3. Reference matter

a. Bibliography
b. Appendixes

The order of the bibliography and appendixes may be reversed if desired.

Some institutions may not require inclusion of all the preliminary pages listed above. Some may require a different sequence. Requirements for the form of the title page, approval page, vita sheet, and abstract may vary. Before preparing these parts, the student should determine the exact requirements of his own institution. The description of these parts given below and the sample pages are recommended as good form, but may not conform to the requirements of some institutions.

D. DESCRIPTION OF THE PARTS

1. Title page

The title page should contain the exact title of the thesis or dissertation, the author's full name, the degree for which it is submitted, the name of the division or department under which the work was conducted, the date submitted, and the name of the university or college. The form and spacing of a title page is shown on page 30.

2. Copyright notice

If a copyright notice is included in a thesis or dissertation, it should be inserted after the title page and neither counted nor numbered in the paging.

A copyright notice is as follows:

Copyright © by
Joseph James Jones
1967

It should be centered near the bottom margin.

By including the symbol © followed by the name of the copyright owner and the year of publication, the author obtains protection in all countries participating in the Universal Copyright Convention as well as in the United States.

3. Approval page

Each copy of the thesis or dissertation must include an approval page signed preferably in permanent black ink by members of the thesis or doctoral committee. The form is shown on page 31.

4. Vita, publications, and fields of study

Some institutions require the authors of doctoral dissertations to include a biographical sheet containing vita (place and date of birth, colleges and dates of degrees, and academic positions), a list of the author's publications, and his fields of study (see page 32).

5. Dedication page

The dedication page in a thesis or dissertation is optional. If included, it consists of "Dedicated to . . . (name or names)" or "To . . ." followed by a comment if the writer chooses.

6. Preface or acknowledgments

A preface should include such matters as the writer's reason for making the study, its scope and purpose, and the aids afforded him in the process of research by institutions and persons. If the writer thinks he has nothing significant to say that has not been covered in the text, the heading "Acknowledgments" rather than "Preface" should be used. The heading is typed in capital letters and centered at least two inches below the top of the page, or more if the text is short. If less than one page in length, the entire preface should be centered on the page.

7. Abstract

Most universities require an abstract of each thesis or dissertation, usually limited to 250 words for a master's thesis and 500 words for a doctoral dissertation. Since requirements concerning length vary in different institutions, the student should determine the exact requirements he will need to meet.

An abstract should include:

a. A statement of the problem
b. An explanation of the methods and procedures used in gathering data
c. A summary of findings

If the doctoral dissertations accepted by the university are sent to University Microfilms, a separate unpaged copy of the abstract is required for publication in *Dissertation Abstracts*. This unpaged copy is in addition to the copies that form a part of the official copies of the dissertation.

The form for an abstract is shown on page 33.

8. Table of contents

The table of contents lists the major divisions of the paper, including the chapters or equivalent divisions, the appendixes, and the bibliography. The preliminaries may be listed if the writer wishes; it is not necessary to include them. The preface may be listed without the other preliminaries.

THE FIGURE OF HERBERT HOOVER

IN THE 1928 CAMPAIGN

A dissertation submitted in partial satisfaction of the

requirements for the degree of Doctor of Philosophy

in History

by

Kent Michael Schofield

January, 1966

University of California, Riverside

The dissertation of Kent Michael Schofield is approved:

_____

_____

_____

_____

_____
Committee Chairman

January, 1966

University of California, Riverside

VITA

August 12, 1936 — Born — Los Angeles, California

1963 — B.S., California State College, Long Beach, California

1963–65 — Teaching Assistant, California State College, Long
    Beach, California

1965–66 — Member, Technical Staff, Aerospace Corporation,
    El Segundo, California

1967–68 — Teaching Assistant, University of California,
    Riverside

1969 — Ph.D. in Chemistry, University of California, Riverside

PUBLICATIONS

D. G. Marsh and J. Heicklen, J. Phys. Chem., 69, 4410
(1965).

D. G. Marsh and J. Heicklen, J. Am. Chem. Soc., 88, 269
(1966).

D. G. Marsh and J. Heicklen, J. Phys. Chem., 70, 3008
(1966).

D. G. Marsh, E. Heine, and J. M. Pitts, Jr., Trans. Faraday
Soc., 64, 2308 (1968).

FIELDS OF STUDY

Physical Chemistry

Photochemistry

Kinetics

THE PHOTOCHEMISTRY OF CYCLOPROPYL KETONES

A dissertation submitted in partial satisfaction of the

requirements for the degree of Doctor of Philosophy

in Chemistry

University of California, Riverside, 1969

by

Dana Gibson Marsh

ABSTRACT

The vapor phase photochemistry of methyl cyclopropyl ketone (I), dicyclopropyl ketone (II), methyl 2, 2-dimethylcyclo-propyl . . . . .

The heading "Table of Contents" or "Contents" is typed in capital letters and centered at least two inches below the top of the sheet. If the table of contents is short, it should be typed lower than two inches. The entire table should be centered on the page.

There should be three spaces between the heading "Table of Contents" and the first entry. Chapter numbers are in capital roman numerals and chapter titles in capital letters. The word "Chapter," with only the first letter capitalized, is typed flush with the left margin, above the column of chapter numbers. If the major divisions of the paper are not called chapters, this designation is omitted in the table of contents. If the designation "Chapter" is not used, it is permissible to omit numbers before the titles of the divisions in the table of contents and in the text. The word "Page," with only the first letter capitalized, is typed flush with the right margin, above the column of page numbers.

The chapter numbers are aligned by the last digit on the right, with the longest number flush with the left margin. The page numbers are also aligned on the right. Periods are used after the chapter numbers but not after the page numbers.

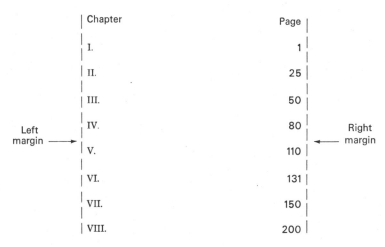

Double-spacing is used between chapter titles. If a chapter title is longer than one line, the second and subsequent lines are indented five spaces from the first line and the lines are double-spaced.

Leaders (double-spaced periods) should extend from the last word of each title to the page number in the column on the right. The leaders should be aligned vertically on the page and should end three spaces before the column of figure numbers.

If the chapters are grouped under parts, there should be three spaces between the heading "Part" and the preceding title. Double spacing is used between "Part" and the first title under it. The heading "Part" should be followed by a capital roman numeral and centered. If titles are used for the parts, they are in capital letters and typed on the same line with "Part" and the numeral. If the title for a part runs to more than one line, it is indented in inverted pyramid form.

Whether or not subdivisions of chapters are listed in the table of contents depends upon the writer. He may wish to present subheadings and thus offer the table of contents as a more or less complete outline of the entire paper. If included, subheadings should be listed two spaces below chapter headings, indented five spaces, and double-spaced. In subheadings, the first letter of the first and last words and of all nouns, pronouns, verbs, adjectives, and adverbs are capitalized.

Sample tables of contents appear on pages 35–37.

TABLE OF CONTENTS

CONTENTS

TABLE OF CONTENTS

9. *List of tables*

If several tables are included in the thesis or dissertation, a list should follow the table of contents. The position of the heading "List of Tables," typed in capital letters, should be the same as for the heading "Table of Contents." The first entry is typed three spaces below the heading. The table titles are double-spaced. If a title is longer than one line, the second and subsequent lines are indented five spaces from the first line and double-spaced.

Table numbers, in arabic numerals, are listed at the left. The word "Table," with only the first letter capitalized, is typed flush with the left margin, above the column of table numbers. The word "Page," with only the first letter capitalized, is typed flush with the right margin, above the column of page numbers. The column of table numbers and the column of page numbers are aligned by the last digits on the right. See section 8 above.

In the titles of tables, the first letter of the first and last words, and of all nouns, pronouns, verbs, adjectives, and adverbs should be capitalized. Leaders (double-spaced periods) should extend from the last word of each title to the page number in the column on the right. The leaders should be aligned vertically and should end three spaces before the column of page numbers (see page 39).

10. *List of illustrations*

If several illustrations are used, a list should follow the list of tables. The list of illustrations should be in the same general form as the list of tables. The word "Figure" should appear above the list of figure numbers at the left. If there is a separately numbered series of one type of illustration such as maps, the listing should be separate and headed with the proper designation.

Plates should be listed separately with roman numerals in the left column and the word "Plate" in capital letters above this column. If there are several plates, a separate page should be used to list them. If there are only a few, they may be listed on the same page with the figures but in a separate grouping.

Sample lists of illustrations are on pages 40–42.

11. *Divisions of the text*

a. Introduction

The text usually begins with an introduction which may be headed either "Introduction" or "Chapter I." "Introduction" may be preferred especially if it is short. It begins on page 1 of the text.

b. Chapters or equivalent divisions

The main body of the text is usually divided into chapters, each with a number and title. If the paper is short, the writer may prefer to omit the word "Chapter" and use capital roman numerals before the headings of the divisions.

If the divisions are designated as *chapters*, the word "Chapter," in capital letters, followed by a capital roman numeral, is centered on a line by itself, two inches from the top edge of the paper. The title of the chapter, in capital letters, is centered three spaces below. If the word "Chapter" is not used, the roman numeral, followed by a period, and the title in capital letters on the same line are centered two inches from the top edge of the paper. If a title is longer than one line, it should be double-spaced and indented in

LIST OF TABLES

LIST OF FIGURES

LIST OF PLATES

LIST OF ILLUSTRATIONS

inverted pyramid form. Three spaces are allowed between the title and the first line of text below it. Each chapter or equivalent section begins on a new page which is numbered at the bottom.

If a paper consists of many chapters, the writer may choose to group them into parts. The parts may or may not have titles. If this arrangement is used, the chapters are numbered in one sequence throughout the paper.

c. Headings for divisions

(1) Centered heading

A heading for a major division of a chapter is centered three spaces below the last line of the preceding section, and underlined for emphasis or not, as desired. If more than one line, the heading should be single-spaced in inverted pyramid form. The first letter of the first and last words, and of all nouns, pronouns, verbs, adjectives, and adverbs should be capitalized. There are three spaces between the centered heading and the following line of text.

(2) Side heading

A second style of heading is the side heading, flush with the left margin, on a separate line, underlined or not, with only the first letter of the first word and proper nouns and proper adjectives capitalized. If a side heading is more than one line, it is single-spaced with each line flush with the left margin. A side heading is three spaces below the last line of the preceding paragraph and two spaces above the following line of text.

(3) Paragraph heading

A third type of heading is the paragraph heading placed at the beginning of the first line of the paragraph, underlined, and followed by a period. Capitalization is the same as in side headings.

(4) Series of headings

If there is only one series of divisions in a chapter, the writer may choose either the centered or side heading. If there are subdivisions of the major divisions of the chapter, centered headings are used for the major divisions and side headings for the subdivisions. If a third series is needed, paragraph headings are used.

```
          STRATIGRAPHY AND PALEONTOLOGY   (chapter title)


              Willow Hole Foundation   (centered heading)


Lithology  (side heading)


     Conglomerates.  The conglomerates make up 20 to 25 percent
of the formation.  (paragraph heading)
```

d. Dissertations in two or more parts

Some dissertations are in two or more separate parts, each with its own title, and each divided into its own series of chapters. See page 45 for a sample title page of a dissertation in two separate parts. The table of contents should list the contents of

Part II immediately following the listing of the contents of Part I. The list of tables and of illustrations for Part II should immediately follow the listing for Part I. Each part should have its own bibliography or list of references. A half title page is recommended before the first page of each part. A half title page consists of the title only, in shortened form if desired, centered on a separate page. The pages should be numbered consecutively throughout the entire dissertation, that is, with only one series of numbers.

e. Conclusions

Conclusions or a summary of the entire thesis may be presented as the last chapter or in a separate section not designated as a chapter. Theses divided into two or more parts may have conclusions or a summary at the end of each part.

12. Bibliography

The heading "Bibliography" is centered two inches below the top of the paper. Three spaces are allowed between the heading and the first entry.

See pages 74–88 for a discussion of the bibliography and examples of form for citations.

13. Appendixes

Appendixes are used to present material which is supplementary to the text, such as schedules and forms used in collecting data, copies of documents, case studies, technical notes, and illustrative material. Each category should form a separate appendix.

Appendixes may or may not have titles. If there are two or more appendixes, they should be numbered or lettered. The heading "Appendix," followed by a number or letter if used, should be centered two inches below the top edge of the paper. If a title is used, it should be in capital letters and centered three spaces below the heading. The text begins three spaces below the title.

E. COPIES

Two copies of theses and dissertations are usually required for deposit in the library of the university or college. In addition to these official copies, the department may require one or more copies. The student may wish to have additional copies made for his own use. The student should investigate the requirements of his institution for the number of copies before preparing the manuscript in final form.

F. PAPER

The official copies for deposit should be on bond paper of 16- or 20-pound weight. This weight is also recommended for all additional copies. Some institutions require special thesis paper for the official copies. Further typing instructions are given on pages 117–120.

G. METHODS OF REPRODUCING COPIES

Copies may be made by either typing carbon copies or reproducing by the xerographic or a lithographic process such as multilith. If carbon copies are used, the original and first carbon copy should be the official copies for deposit.

I. EXCITED STATE INTERACTIONS AND ENERGY TRANSFER

IN PYRENE MOLECULAR CRYSTALS

II. THE QUENCHING OF ORGANIC TRIPLET STATES BY

MOLECULAR OXYGEN

A dissertation submitted in partial satisfaction of the

requirements for the degree of Doctor of Philosophy

in Chemistry

by

Kenji Kawaoka

December, 1967

University of California, Riverside

Two reproducing processes commonly used are multilith and xerography. Of these two processes, multilith is more economical for more than five copies. It also produces cleaner and sharper copies. If this process is used, the manuscript is typed either (1) directly on multilith stencils or (2) on bond paper, from which multilith stencils are prepared by a photographic process. The manuscript should be carefully typed with a minimum of erasures in order that neat copies may be produced.

The xerographic process is recommended for five or fewer copies. Copies are made directly from the original typed copy. If this process is used, the original typed copy is usually required for the first official copy for deposit.

Printing is usually considered too expensive for theses and dissertations.

Processes which are usually not considered acceptable include ditto, hectograph, mimeograph, and thermofax.

The student should find out which processes are accepted or required by his own institution before preparing the manuscript in final form.

For best results sufficient time should be allowed for careful typing and for the reproducing of additional copies.

Many universities and colleges have a department of photographic services on the campus. If the student does not have access to such services in his institution, he may consult a commercial printer concerning the processes mentioned above.

H. PUBLICATION BY UNIVERSITY MICROFILMS

Many universities send a copy of all doctoral dissertations accepted by their institutions to University Microfilms, Inc., Ann Arbor, Michigan. University Microfilms reproduces dissertations in microfilm and xerographic form and makes them available for purchase. This constitutes publication. The author's abstract, sent with the complete copy of the dissertation, is published in *Dissertation Abstracts*. The order number and prices for microfilm and xerographic copies of the complete dissertation are listed with the abstract.

The author signs an agreement form supplied by University Microfilms through the university's graduate office or another agency of the campus. He thereby permits the reproduction and sale of his dissertation. University Microfilms deposits one positive microfilm copy in the Library of Congress. The dissertation is then listed in the author and subject catalogs of the Library of Congress. The author retains rights to publish or sell the dissertation in any form except by reproduction from a negative microfilm as described in the University Microfilms agreement.

If the author of a dissertation quotes extensively or reproduces tables or illustrative material from a published work, he must obtain permission from the copyright owner to use this material. The University Microfilms agreement form includes a statement that the dissertation does not infringe upon any statutory or common law copyright and that the author is legally responsible for any infringement.

If the author wishes to copyright the dissertation, he may fill out the appropriate parts of the agreement form. University Microfilms will file the copyright application in the author's name and deposit two positive microfilm copies in the U.S. Copyright Office. Payment of a fee is required to cover this service. The author will not be able to obtain a copyright of the dissertation at a later date unless it has been copyrighted at the time of publication by University Microfilms.

The office of the graduate division of a university usually handles the arrangements between the student and University Microfilms.

Further information concerning these arrangements may be obtained from the graduate division of the university or by addressing an inquiry to: Supervisor, Manuscript Publications, University Microfilms, 300 North Zeeb Road, Ann Arbor, Michigan, 48106.

I. COPYRIGHT

The procedure for obtaining a copyright on a doctoral dissertation through University Microfilms is explained in the preceding section. If the author wishes to publish all or parts of his dissertation before it is submitted to University Microfilms, he notifies the graduate office of his institution to withhold sending it to University Microfilms, usually for a period of a year. He obtains the copyright directly from the Register of Copyrights. He indicates on the University Microfilms agreement form that the dissertation has been copyrighted and enters on this form the copyright notice as it appears in the published edition. This notice should also be included in the copy of the dissertation submitted to University Microfilms.

To copyright a doctoral dissertation, master's thesis, or other work, the author should write to the Register of Copyrights, Copyright Office, Library of Congress, Washington, D.C. 20540, to obtain information and application forms.

III
Documentation

The treatment of documentation in this section applies to the humanities and social sciences fields. The special forms of documentation for the biological and physical sciences fields are treated in a separate section, pages 107–116.

The two forms of documentation in research papers are footnotes and bibliography. Footnotes are primarily for the purpose of acknowledging or identifying quotations, statements, or ideas taken from another author. They are also used to substantiate statements by citing the source of information used. They cite a specific page or pages of a work. The bibliography is a listing of sources used in the preparation of the paper. It cites entire books, articles, or other works.

A. FOOTNOTES

1. Types of footnotes

a. *Reference footnotes.* Footnotes used for the purpose of documentation, as described in the paragraph above, are reference footnotes. The first time a work is cited, full bibliographic information must be given as explained and illustrated in this section.

b. *Content footnotes.* Another type of footnote is the content footnote, which is used for explanatory material not of sufficient importance or too interruptive or incidental to be included in the text. See page 111 for an example.

A content footnote may include a reference to a work, but its primary purpose is for explanatory comment.

```
    Gabriel A. Almond's more inclusive functional analysis in
Politics in the Developing Areas (Princeton, N.J.: Princeton
University Press, 1960) identifies additional theoretical
variables.
```

c. *Cross references.* Footnotes may be used for references to other pages of the paper, either to the text or to content footnotes. Cross references may not be used as substitutes for reference footnotes.

```
    See above (or below), p. 30.
    See footnote 21, p. 48.
```

2. *Reducing the number of footnotes*

Excessive footnoting should be avoided. The writer should consider including some explanatory statements in the text, if they are not too interruptive, rather than using a large number of content footnotes. It is sometimes possible to combine two or more references in one footnote instead of using a separate note for each reference, as illustrated in the statement from the text and footnote below. Semicolons are used to separate the references.

```
    The concept of group conflict is considered in detail
by Lewis A. Coser and Ralf Dahrendorf.1
```

```
    1Lewis A. Coser, Functions of Social Conflict (Glencoe:
Free Press, 1956); Ralf Dahrendorf, Class and Class Conflict in
Industrial Society (Palo Alto: Stanford University Press, 1959).
```

3. *Numbering*

Footnotes are numbered consecutively throughout the paper, or, if the paper is very long, throughout each chapter or section. The quotation or statement used in the text is followed by an arabic numeral typed slightly above the line (superscript). The same numeral, also superscript, appears at the beginning of the footnote at the bottom of the same page on which the quotation or statement appears. Superscript numerals follow marks of punctuation in the text with no space between. No marks of punctuation are used after superscript numerals. See page 18 for examples.

If content footnotes are used, they are numbered in the same sequence with reference footnotes. If cross references are given in footnotes, they are also numbered in the same sequence.

4. *Placement*

Notes in a research paper are usually placed at the bottom of pages. An alternate method is to place all the notes at the end of the paper. In a long paper, they may be placed at the end of each chapter. If they are placed at the bottom of the pages, they are footnotes. If they are placed at the end of the paper or chapters, they should be headed "Notes."

It is recommended that notes be placed at the bottom of the pages containing references to them in research papers in the humanities and social sciences fields.

Notes for a manuscript submitted for publication should be typed on a separate sheet or sheets and double spaced both within and between notes.

5. *Indention and spacing*

The text and the footnotes are separated by an unbroken line ten spaces long extending from the left margin one double space below the text. The first line of the footnote material is one double space below this line.

Footnotes should be in paragraph form. The first line is indented five spaces from the left margin and the second and subsequent lines are flush with the left margin. Single-spacing should be used within footnotes and double-spacing between footnotes.

A page containing footnotes must be planned so that footnotes do not run into the lower margin or to the next page. See the typing instructions, page 118, and examples, pages 17–24.

6. *Capitalization of titles of books, articles, periodicals, and other publications*

a. English

In English titles, the first and last words and all nouns, pronouns, adjectives, adverbs, and verbs are capitalized. The first word following a colon is capitalized.

b. German

In German titles, the first word and all nouns and words used as nouns, and adjectives derived from names of persons are capitalized. See footnotes 40 and 70.

c. French, Italian, Spanish

In French, Italian, and Spanish titles, only the first word and proper nouns are capitalized. Adjectives derived from proper nouns are not capitalized. If the first word is an article, the first letter of the noun following is also capitalized. See footnotes 41, 42, 43, 71, 72, and 73.

d. Russian

In transliterated Russian titles, only the first word and proper nouns are capitalized. In an English translation following the Russian title, the first word, proper nouns, and adjectives derived from proper nouns are capitalized. See footnotes 44 and 45.

e. Latin and Greek

In Latin and Greek titles, the first word, proper nouns, and adjectives derived from proper nouns are capitalized. See footnotes 46, 47, 48, 49, and 50.

7. *Punctuation*

Punctuation within footnotes is explained in detail in the discussion of footnote references to various types of material.

8. *Books*

Footnote references to books should include:

a. Author's full name
b. Title, including subtitle, if any
c. Editor, translator, illustrator, author of preface, if any
d. Series and number, if any
e. Edition, if other than the first
f. Number of volumes, if applicable
g. Facts of publication (place, publisher, date)
h. Volume number, if any
i. Page number.

a. Author

The author's name is given in normal order. The first name is spelled out if known. The initial only is usually given for the second name (John J. Jones). If the first name cannot be found, initials may be given for both names. Initials are acceptable for authors who use only their initials, such as T. S. Eliot. A comma separates the author's name from the title.

If there are two authors, both names are given in the citation. If there are three authors, all the names are given, with a comma following each name. If there are four or more authors, the first name only is given, followed by *et al.* or the English equivalent *and others. Et al.* is underlined because it is an abbreviation of a foreign phrase (*et alii*).

(1) One author

    ¹Robert A. Nisbet, The Sociological Tradition (New York: Basic Books, 1966), p. 125.

(2) Two authors

    ²W. T. Easterbrook and Hugh G. J. Aitken, Canadian Economic History (Toronto: Macmillan Company of Canada, 1956), p. 500.

(3) Three authors

    ³Paul H. Sheats, Clarence D. Jayne, and Ralph B. Spence, Adult Education: The Community Approach (New York: Dryden Press, 1953), p. 410.

(4) Four or more authors

    ⁴Robert K. Carr, et al., American Democracy in Theory and Practice, 3d ed. (New York: Holt, Rinehart and Winston, 1960), p. 810.

(5) Pseudonymous author

If a pseudonym appears on the title page of a book, the author's real name, if known, should be given first with the pseudonym following in brackets.

    ⁵William S. Porter [O. Henry], Sixes and Sevens (Garden City, N.Y.: Doubleday, Page & Company, 1920), p. 10.

If a writer is better known by his pseudonym than by his real name, the pseudonym is given first with the real name following in brackets.

    ⁶George Eliot [Marian Evans], Middlemarch (London: Zodiac Press, 1950), p. 101.

If only the pseudonym is known, it is given as the author followed by "pseud." in brackets.

    ⁷Taylor Caldwell [pseud.], The Arm and the Darkness (New York: Charles Scribner's Sons, 1943), p. 89.

(6) Anonymous work

A work which has no known author or editor is cited by title.

⁸<u>Song of Roland</u>, trans. by Leonard Bacon (New Haven, Conn.: Yale University Press, 1914), p. 19.

If there is no author's name on the title page, but the author is known, his name is given in brackets before the title.

⁹[Thomas P. Prest], <u>The Smuggler King or the Foundling of the Wreck: A Nautico Domestic Romance</u> (London: E. Lloyd, 1844), p. 31.

(7) Editor as author

If a book has an editor in place of an author, the name is followed by *ed.*, or *eds.* for plural, set off by commas.

¹⁰Philip E. Wheelwright, ed., <u>The Presocratics</u> (New York: Odyssey Press, 1966), p. 297.

(8) Compiler as author

If a book has a compiler in place of an author, the name is followed by *comp.*, or *comps.* for plural, set off by commas.

¹¹Jack D. Mezirow and Dorothea Berry, comps., <u>The Literature of Liberal Adult Education, 1945–1957</u> (New York: Scarecrow Press, 1960), p. 102.

(9) Society, association, or institution as author

¹²Governmental Affairs Institute, Washington, D.C., <u>America at the Polls: A Handbook of American Presidential Election Statistics 1920–1964</u>, comp. and ed. by Richard M. Scammon (Pittsburgh: University of Pittsburgh Press, 1965), p. 23.

¹³American Sociological Association, <u>Directory, Constitution and By–Laws</u> (Washington, D.C.: American Sociological Association, 1967), p. 315.

b. Title

The title of a book should be given as it appears on the title page. If there is a subtitle, it should be included in the first reference to the book.

The complete title, including the subtitle if there is one, should be underlined. Both the title and subtitle should be capitalized according to the rules on page 51.

If there is punctuation within the title as it appears on the title page, this punctuation should be followed. It is sometimes necessary to add punctuation. For example, a subtitle usually appears on a separate line from the title. In a footnote reference, a colon should be added to separate the title from the subtitle. A comma is used at the end of the title unless the facts of publication enclosed in parentheses follow immediately.

¹⁴John L. Beatty, <u>Warwick and Holland: Being the Lives of Robert and Henry Rich</u> (Denver: Alan Swallow, 1965), p. 180.

If a title is unusually long, it is permissible to omit part of it and indicate the omission by three spaced periods.

15Frederick S. Merryweather, <u>Bibliomania in the Middle Ages, Being Sketches of Bookworms, Collectors, Bible Students, Scribes, and Illuminators from the Anglo-Saxon and Norman Periods, to the Introduction of Printing in England</u>. . . Rev. ed. (London: Woodstock Press, 1933), p. 56.

A title within a title is enclosed in quotation marks.

16Abbie F. Potts, <u>Shakespeare and "The Faerie Queene"</u> (Ithaca, N.Y.: Cornell University Press, 1958), p. 250.

c. Editor, translator, illustrator, author of preface

If a work has both an author and an editor, the author's name is given first and the editor's name follows the title. The name of a translator or illustrator also follows the title.

17William Wordsworth, <u>Literary Criticism</u>, ed. by Paul M. Zall (Lincoln: University of Nebraska Press, 1966), p. 53.

18Jean Baptiste Racine, <u>Phaedra</u>, trans. by John Cairncross (Geneva: Librairie E. Droz, 1958), p. 102.

19Kathleen Arnott, <u>African Myths and Legends</u>, illus. by Joan Kiddell-Monroe (New York: H. Z. Walck, 1963), p. 178.

Note that *edited, translated,* and *illustrated* are abbreviated.

If the title page indicates that the book contains a preface or introduction by a well-known person, that information is given after the title.

20Paul Laurence Dunbar, <u>Lyrics of Lowly Life</u>, with an introduction by W. D. Howells (New York: Dodd, Mead and Company, 1906), p. 26.

d. Series

If a book is part of a series, the title of the series is given following the title of the book. A series title is capitalized according to the rules for capitalization of titles of books. It is not underlined. A comma separates the title of the book from the title of the series.

If the publications in a series are numbered, the number is given after the series title. Some series have volume numbers; some have publication numbers; some have both volume and publication numbers; some have numbers only, without indication of volume or number; and some series are not numbered.

21Theodore H. Von Laue, <u>Leopold Ranke: The Formative Years</u>, Princeton Studies in History, vol. 4 (Princeton, N.J.: Princeton University Press, 1950), p. 98.

22Alfred L. Kroeber, <u>The Seri</u>, Southwest Museum Papers, no. 6 (Los Angeles: Southwest Museum, 1931), p. 15.

²³Leslie Spier, <u>Plains Indian Parfleche Designs</u>, University of Washington Publications in Anthropology, vol. 4, no. 3 (Seattle: University of Washington Press, 1931), p. 299.

²⁴Robert V. Hine, <u>Edward Kern and American Expansion</u>, Yale Western Americana Series, 1 (New Haven, Conn.: Yale University Press, 1962), p. 57.

²⁵John G. Davies, <u>Early Christian Church</u>, History of Religion Series, ed. by E. O. James (New York: Holt, Rinehart and Winston, 1965), p. 89.

e. Edition

If the edition of a book is other than the first, this is usually indicated by the number of the edition. In footnotes the edition number is given in arabic numerals after the title and is preceded by a comma. If the number of the edition does not appear on the title page of the book, it can be taken from the verso of the title page.

²⁶John C. Weaver and Fred E. Lukermann, <u>World Resource Statistics</u>, 2d ed. (Minneapolis: Burgess Publishing Co., 1953), p. 150.

If the edition is indicated as revised but no number is given, the abbreviation *rev. ed.* is used.

²⁷Edwin T. Coman, Jr., <u>Sources of Business Information</u>, rev. ed. (Berkeley and Los Angeles: University of California Press, 1964), p. 19.

If a number is given plus the words *revised* or *enlarged* or both, this information is included in abbreviated form.

²⁸Robert L. Collison, <u>Bibliographies, Subject and National: A Guide to Their Contents, Arrangement and Use</u>, 2d ed. rev. and enl. (New York: Hafner Publishing Co., 1962), p. 3.

If the title page indicates a person other than the author has been responsible for the revision, his name also appears in the citation.

²⁹Henry W. Fowler, <u>A Dictionary of Modern English Usage</u>, 2d ed. rev. by Sir Ernest Gowers (Oxford: At the Clarendon Press, 1965), p. 543.

If a reprint edition is used, both the original publisher and date and the publisher and date of the reprint edition may be given.

³⁰Thomas W. Field, <u>An Essay toward an Indian Bibliography: Being a Catalogue of Books Relating to the History, Antiquities, Languages, Customs, Religion, Wars, Literature and Origin of the American Indians</u>. . . (New York: Scribner, Armstrong and Co., 1873; reprint ed., Columbus, Ohio: Long's College Book Co., 1951), p. 53.

It is also permissible to give the date only of the original publication omitting place and publisher (1873; reprint ed., Columbus, Ohio: Long's College Book Co., 1951), or to give place, publisher, and date of the original publication and the date only of the reprint edition (New York: Scribner, Armstrong and Co., 1873; reprint ed., 1951).

f. Number of volumes

If a work in more than one volume, under one author and title, is cited in its entirety, the total number of volumes precedes the facts of publication.

> [31]Amos J. Peaslee, <u>International Governmental Organiza-</u><u>tions: Constitutional Documents</u>, 2d ed. rev., 2 vols. (The Hague: Martinus Nijhoff, 1961).

If a specific passage is cited, the volume number in roman numerals and the page number in arabic numerals follow the facts of publication.

> [32]Amos J. Peaslee, <u>International Governmental Organiza-</u><u>tions: Constitutional Documents</u>, 2d ed. rev. (The Hague: Martinus Nijhoff, 1961), II, 23.

The number of volumes precedes the facts of publication in a work published over a period of two or more years whether the work is cited in its entirety or a specific passage from one volume is cited.

> [33]Robert Southey, <u>Life and Correspondence of Robert</u> <u>Southey</u>, ed. by Charles C. Southey, 6 vols. (London: Longman, Brown, Green, and Longmans, 1849–1850).

> [34]Robert Southey, <u>Life and Correspondence of Robert</u> <u>Southey</u>, ed. by Charles C. Southey, 6 vols. (London: Longman, Brown, Green, and Longmans, 1849–1850), II, 63.

g. Facts of publication

The facts of publication include place (city, city and state, or city and country), publisher, and date (year). These items are enclosed in parentheses in footnotes. A colon is used after the place, a comma after the publisher, and a comma after the second parenthesis.

(1) Place

If several places of publication are given with a publisher's name on the title page, the first place only is given. If two cities are given with a publisher's name, it is permissible, but not necessary, to include both in the reference.

> (New York: McGraw-Hill Book Company, 1968)

> (Chicago and London: University of Chicago Press, 1969)

If a city is well known, it is not necessary to include the state or country.

> (Boston: Houghton Mifflin Company, 1948)

> (Paris: Gallimard, 1927)

If the state is included in the publisher's name, it is not necessary to give the state after the city.

(Lincoln: University of Nebraska Press, 1966)

If the city is not well known, the abbreviation of the state, province, or country should be used.

(Belmont, Calif.:   Wadsworth Publishing Co., 1967)

(Sudbury, Ont.:   D. & H. Schroeder, 1966)

If there are two or more cities by the same name, the abbreviation of the state should be used.

(Springfield, Mass.:   G. & C. Merriam Company, 1961)

If a book was published in a foreign city, the anglicized form of the name should be used, such as Munich for München, Milan for Milano, and Brussels for Bruxelles.

If there is no place of publication given on the title page, the abbreviation *n.p.* for *no place* is used.

(2) Publisher

The name of the publisher may be given in full as it appears on the title page of the book, or in abbreviated form.

McGraw-Hill Book Company or McGraw-Hill

R. R. Bowker Co. or Bowker

If the full form is used, abbreviations on the title page should be followed, such as *Co.* for *Company* and *Bros.* for *Brothers. The* at the beginning of a publisher's name is omitted. *Inc.* and *Ltd.* are usually omitted.

In some disciplines, the name of the publisher is omitted in references. Only the place and date, separated by a comma, are given in the facts of publication.

(Boston, 1968)

The student should determine which form is preferred or required by the department for which he is writing a paper. If material is being prepared for publication, the practice of the publishing company or journal concerned should be followed. One style must be followed consistently throughout a paper, article, or book.

The full names of publishers are given in the examples in this section. If an alternate style is used, the necessary adaptations can be made.

If a book was copublished by two publishers, both are included.

(New York: G. P. Putnam's Sons; London: Everett and Co., 1907)

If the title page indicates a book was published by the subsidiary of a publisher, both names are included.

(New York: Plenum Publishing Corp., Da Capo Press, 1968)

If the name of a publisher has changed, the name should be given as it appears on the title page of the book cited, not in its present form.

Doubleday, Page and Company (now Doubleday & Company)

Henry Holt & Co. (now Holt, Rinehart and Winston)

If a book was published for an institution or society, this name is included with the publisher's name.

35Robert H. Lowie, Indians of the Plains, Anthropological Handbook, no. 1 (New York: Published for the American Museum of Natural History by McGraw-Hill Book Company, 1954), p. 101.

For inclusion of publishers in a reference to a reprint edition, see pages 55–56.

The name of a foreign publisher should not be translated, although the place of publication is given in anglicized form.

(Milan: Istituto Editoriale Cisalpino, 1951)

If no publisher is given, the abbreviation *n.p.* is used. This abbreviation is also used for no place of publication. If neither place nor publisher is given, the one abbreviation *n.p.* stands for both.

(n.p., 1962)

(3) Date

The date of publication should be taken from the title page. If there is no date on the title page, the copyright date should be taken from the verso of the title page (copyright page). If there is more than one copyright date, the latest should be used. A date on the copyright page indicating a reprinting, but not a new edition, should not be used.

If a work in more than one volume was published over a period of two or more years, the inclusive dates are given. If a multivolume work is still in progress, a dash is used after the date (1960–   ).

If no date is given, the abbreviation *n.d.* is used. If the publication date is found elsewhere than on the title page or verso, it is enclosed in brackets.

(New York: Hawthorn Books, n.d.)

(New York: Hawthorn Books, [1929])

h. Volume number

If a volume number is cited following the facts of publication, it is given in capital roman numerals. It is preceded by a comma and followed by a comma before the page number. If both volume and page are given after the facts of publication, the abbreviations for volume and page are omitted. See footnote 32.

i. Page number

Page numbers are indicated with arabic numerals. The abbreviations *p.* and *pp.* for plural are used before the numbers except when a volume number immediately precedes the page number as explained above.

If two or more consecutive pages are cited, inclusive paging should be given rather than one number followed by *ff.* (pp. 15–22, not 15ff.).

In citing inclusive paging, two digits should be given for the second number of a two-, three-, or four-digit series (pp. 50–55, not pp. 50–5; pp. 160–65, not pp. 160–5; pp. 2115–19, not pp. 2115–9). Exceptions are numbers including zeros (pp. 108–9, not pp. 108–09; pp. 1007–8, not pp. 1007–08). The zero is not repeated. Three digits should be given for the second number of a three-digit series in which the first digit of the second number is higher than the first digit of the first number (pp. 189–210, not pp. 189–10). In longer numbers, as many digits as are necessary for clarity should be included in the second number (pp. 1598–1611, not pp. 1598–11; pp. 1989–2012, not pp. 1989–12).

9. *References to special types of books*

a. Multivolume works

(1) A multivolume work with one author and title, published in one year

One volume of a multivolume work which has one author and one title for all volumes, published in one year, is cited by giving the number of the particular volume after the facts of publication. The volume number is indicated by a roman numeral, and the page by an arabic numeral. When both volume and page numbers follow the facts of publication, the abbreviations *vol.* and *p.* are omitted.

[36]Margaret H. Bulley, <u>Art and Everyman: Basis for Appreciation</u> (London: B. T. Batsford, 1952), I, 5.

(2) A multivolume work with one author and one title for all volumes, published over a period of two or more years

The total number of volumes is given before the facts of publication. The inclusive dates of publication are given. The particular volume cited follows the facts of publication.

[37]Robert Southey, <u>Life and Correspondence of Robert Southey</u>, ed. by Charles C. Southey, 6 vols. (London: Longman, Brown, Green, and Longmans, 1849–50), I, 53.

(3) A multivolume work with one author and title for the complete work, and a separate title for each volume

The number and title of the particular volume cited are given after the title of the complete work. A colon is used after the volume number. The date of publication of the volume cited only is given.

[38]Sir Winston L. S. Churchill, <u>The Second World War</u>, Vol. I: <u>The Gathering Storm</u> (Boston: Houghton Mifflin Company, 1948), p. 532.

(4) A multivolume work with one title and editor for the complete work and a different author and title for each volume

The author and title of the individual volume cited are given first, followed by the volume number, and the title and editor of the complete work. The total number of volumes in the work is given before the facts of publication. Inclusive dates of publication of the complete work are given if the volumes have been published over a period of two or more years. In the following example all volumes were published the same year.

[39]Tucker Brooke, <u>The Renaissance (1500-1660)</u>, Vol. II of <u>Literary History of England</u>, ed. by Albert C. Baugh, 4 vols. (New York: Appleton-Century-Crofts, 1948), p. 95.

b. Foreign works

(1) German

[40]Reinhard Baumgart, <u>Das Ironische und die Ironie in den Werken Thomas Manns</u> (Munich: Carl Hanser Verlag, 1964), p. 132.

(2) French

[41]Raymond Lebèque, <u>Ronsard, l'homme et l'oeuvre</u> (Paris: Hatier-Boivin, 1957), p. 102.

(3) Italian

[42]Antonio Viscardi, <u>La Letteratura italiana dalle origini ai giorni nostri</u> (Milan: Istituto Editoriale Cisalpino, 1951), p. 607.

(4) Spanish

[43]Angel Valbuena Prat, <u>Historia del teatro español</u> (Barcelona: Editorial Noguer, 1956), p. 21.

(5) Russian

Titles of Russian works are transliterated.

[44]Valerii I. Kirpotin, <u>Dostoevskii i Belinskii</u> (Moscow: Sovetskoi Pisatel, 1960), p. 152.

If titles are long, or not readily translated, the English translation of the title in brackets, but not underlined, follows the transliterated Russian title.

[45]Moscow, Akademiia Obshchestvennykh Nauk, <u>Russkaia progressivnaia filosofskaia mysl dvadtsatogo veka</u> [Russian progressive philosophical thought of the twentieth century] (Moscow: VPSh, 1959), p. 28.

c. Classical works

References to Greek and Latin classical works consist only of the author's name, title of the work, and divisions (book, section, lines). No punctuation is used after the author or after the title of the work. The title is underlined. The divisions of a work are indicated with arabic numerals. The numerals indicating different levels of division are separated by periods. A dash is used to indicate inclusive numbers, as for more than one line.

In a paper containing many classical references it is permissible to abbreviate both author and title according to the abbreviations listed in the *Oxford Classical Dictionary*.

[46]Cicero De natura deorum 1.26

or

[46]Cic. Nat. D. 1.26

[47]Virgil Aeneid 2.13–20

or

[47]Verg. Aen. 2.13–20

[48]Ovid Metamorphoses 12.598–606

or

[48]Ov. Met. 12.598–606

[49]Homer Odyssey 3.404–10

or

[49]Hom. Od. 3.404–10

[50]Aristotle Ethica Nicomachea 1.6.12

or

[50]Arist. Eth. Nic. 1.6.12

The facts of publication are omitted since classical works have been published in many editions. The reference in shortened form is useful in locating a passage in any edition.

If a page reference is given in a classical citation, the edition must be indicated following the title. In this type of citation the place and date are also included.

[51]Aristotle, Nicomachean Ethics, Loeb Classical Library (London, 1926), p. 21.

d. Medieval works

References to medieval works may also be given in the shortened form described above for references to classical works.

[52]Aelfric De temporibus anni 3.8–14

[53]Beowulf 1.371–76

e. Biblical references

A biblical reference includes the name of the book, chapter number, and verse number. The name of the book is not underlined. If the name is long, it should be abbreviated. Arabic numerals are used for both chapter and verse numbers. The two numbers are separated by a colon.

[54]John 3:16.

[55]Eccles. 3:1–8.

[56]2 Cor. 7:1.

f. References to separately published plays and poems

A classic play or poem may be cited in a short form similar to that used for Greek and Roman classics. See page 61.

In references to classic plays, capital roman numerals are used for act numbers, small roman numerals for scene numbers, and arabic numerals for lines.

[57]Shakespeare Julius Caesar III. ii. 79–112.

An alternate style is the use of arabic numerals for all divisions.

[57]Shakespeare Julius Caesar 3. 2. 79–112.

In references to classic poems, small roman numerals are used for books or cantos and arabic numerals for lines, or as an alternate style, arabic numerals for all divisions.

[58]Pope Rape of the Lock iii. 5–8.

or

[58]Pope Rape of the Lock 3. 5–8.

References to modern plays and poems include full bibliographic information.

[59]Eugene O'Neill, The Iceman Cometh (New York: Random House, 1946), p. 25.

[60]Edna St. Vincent Millay, Renascence and Other Poems (New York: Harper & Brothers, 1917), p. 14.

10. Component part of a book

If one part is cited from a book made up of several sections or chapters, each by a different author, the author and title of the part cited are given first, followed by the word *in* before the title and editor of the whole book. The title of the part is enclosed in quotation marks. The title of the whole book is underlined.

[61]Stow Persons, "The Origins of the Gentry," in Essays in History and Literature, ed. by Robert H. Bremner (Columbus: Ohio State University Press, 1966), p. 92.

[62]Otis D. Duncan, "The Future Population of the Great Plains," in <u>Symposium on the Great Plains of North America</u>, ed. by Carle C. Zimmerman and Seth Russell (Fargo: North Dakota Institute for Regional Studies, 1967), p. 55.

11. *Encyclopedia articles*

References to articles in encyclopedias include:

a. Author of the article
b. Title of the article, in quotation marks
c. Title of the encyclopedia, underlined
d. Date, if no edition number appears on the title page
e. Volume number, in capital roman numerals
f. Page number, in arabic numerals

Place and publisher are omitted. If an edition number is given, as in footnote 65 the year is omitted. The abbreviations *vol.* and *p.* are not used.

(1) Article with an author

[63]George T. Dickie, "Aesthetics," <u>Encyclopedia Americana</u>, 1967, I, 234.

(2) Article with no author

[64]"Maronites," <u>Collier's Encyclopedia</u>, 1968, XVI, 441.

(3) Article from an encyclopedia with an edition number

[65]James Bryce, "Justinian I," <u>Encyclopaedia Britannica</u>, 11th ed., XV, 596.

12. *Articles in periodicals*

Footnote references to articles in periodicals should include:

a. Author's full name
b. Title of the article
c. Title of the periodical
d. Series, if any
e. Volume number
f. Issue number (usually optional)
g. Date
h. Page number

a. Author

The author's name is given in normal order and is followed by a comma. See page 52 for the use of initials and for two or more authors.

b. Title of article

The title of the article is enclosed in quotation marks and is followed by a comma.

c. Title of the periodical

The title of the periodical is underlined and is followed by a comma. Capitalization of article and periodical titles should be according to the rules on page 51.

d. Series

If a periodical has been issued in more than one series, this is indicated following the title of the periodical by the number of the series, as *2d ser.* or *n.s.* for *new series* or *o.s.* for *old series.*

e. Volume number

It is recommended that the volume number be given in capital roman numerals to make it easily distinguishable from the page number. Some writers and publishers prefer arabic numerals for volume numbers. A different typeface can be used in printed material to distinguish between volume and page numbers, but in typed papers prepared for schools this distinction can best be made by using roman numerals for volume numbers and arabic numerals for page numbers. The abbreviation *vol.* is not used before the volume number in references to periodical articles.

Volume numbers are not necessary in references to daily or weekly publications. They are identified by date only. See footnote 69.

f. Issue number

The issue number, if included, follows the volume number and is separated from it by a comma. If the issue number is included, it is permissible to omit the month or season from the date. It is also permissible to include volume, issue number, and complete date.

```
XLIV (Spring, 1955), 425

XLIV, No. 3 (1955), 425

XLIV, No. 3 (Spring, 1955), 425
```

One of the three forms should be followed consistently. The first form shown above is the most commonly used.

g. Date

The date of the issue cited is enclosed in parentheses, except in a citation which does not include a volume number. No mark of punctuation immediately precedes the first parenthesis. A comma follows the second parenthesis. Inclusion of the month or season in the date varies as explained above under Issue Number. If paging is consecutive throughout a volume, it is permissible to give the year only as in footnote 73. If the day of the month is included, as in footnote 69, the month is abbreviated.

h. Page numbers

Arabic numerals are used for page numbers. The abbreviations *p.* and *pp.* are not used in citations of periodical articles, except when no volume number is given, as in footnote 69.

The place of publication and name of the publisher are not included in citations of periodical articles.

(1) Article with an author

66David S. McLellan, "The North African in France," <u>Yale Review</u>, XLIX (Spring, 1955), 425.

(2) Article with no author

67"ASEE—Ford Foundation Residencies Program," <u>School and Society</u>, XCVII (January, 1969), 10.

(3) Article from a periodical which has been published in more than one series

68Benjamin Rowland, "The World's Image in Indian Architecture," <u>Asian Review</u>, n.s. II (April, 1965), 5.

(4) Article from a weekly periodical

69"Japan in Search of Japan," <u>Newsweek</u>, Nov. 25, 1968, p. 54.

(5) Articles in foreign languages

70Guenther C. Rimbach, "Illusionsperspektiven in der modernen Lyrik," <u>Germanisch—Romanische Monatsschrift</u>, XIV (Oktober, 1964), 371.

71Jean Dagen, "Pour une histoire de la pensée de Fontenelle," <u>Revue d'histoire littéraire de la France</u>, LXVI (Octobre—Décembre, 1966), 620.

72Guido Gonella, "Aspectos negativos del sincretismo y del pragmatismo políticos," <u>Revista de estudios políticos</u>, CLVI (Novembre—Diciembre, 1967), 5.

73Donato Gagliardi, "Cicerone e il neoterismo," <u>Rivista di filologia e di istruzione classica</u>, 3d ser., XCVI (1968), 269.

13. Book reviews

References to book reviews are similar in form to references to periodical articles. Items included are:

Name of the reviewer
Title of the article, if any, in quotation marks
The words *review of*

Title of the book reviewed, underlined
Author of the book reviewed
Title of the periodical, underlined
Series, if any
Volume
Date
Page

[74]Donald J. Greene, review of <u>Johnsonian and Other Essays and Reviews</u>, by R. W. Chapman, <u>Review of English Studies</u>, n.s. V (July, 1954), 332.

[75]Frank Altschul, "Doubting Thomas Diplomacy," review of <u>Between War and Peace</u>, by Herbert Feis, <u>Saturday Review</u>, Oct. 1, 1960, p. 21.

In footnote 75, the date is not enclosed in parentheses and the abbreviation for page is used because no volume number is given in a citation to a weekly publication. See explanation on page 64.

14. *Newspaper articles*

Footnote references to newspaper articles should include:

a. Author's name, if given
b. Title of article
c. Title of newspaper
d. City, if not part of the title of the newspaper
e. Date
f. Section, if applicable
g. Page number
h. Column number (optional)

a. Author

The author's name is given in normal order. A comma is used after the author's name.

b. Title of article

The title of the article is enclosed in quotation marks. A comma is used after the title. If no author's name appears with the article, the citation begins with the title of the article.

c. Title of newspaper

The title of the newspaper is underlined and is followed by a comma.

d. City

If the name of the city in which the newspaper is published is not a part of the title, it is given in parentheses following the title. See footnote 77. Exceptions are well-known newspapers such as *Christian Science Monitor* and *Wall Street Journal*.

e. Date

The date of publication includes day, month, and year. The name of the month is abbreviated since the day of the month is included.

f. Section

If a newspaper is published in several sections, separately paged, the number of the section, in arabic numerals, should be included.

g. Page number

The page number, in arabic numerals, should be included in any citation of a newspaper article.

h. Column number

The inclusion of the column number in the citation is helpful for locating the article. Its inclusion, however, is optional.

An unsigned article may be cited in a shortened form which includes only the name of the newspaper, date, and page.

[76]Fred M. Hechinger, "Schools vs. Riots," New York Times, July 30, 1967, sec. 4, p. 7, col. 3.

[77]"Medical Briefs Urge Expansion," Globe and Mail (Toronto), Aug. 28, 1965, p. 8.

or

[77]Globe and Mail (Toronto), Aug. 28, 1965, p. 8.

15. Pamphlets

References to pamphlets are given in the same forms that are used for references to books. Many pamphlets are published in series. They should be cited according to sample footnotes 21–25.

16. Government publications

In the citation of a government publication, the name of the country, state, city, or other government district is given first, followed by the name of the agency, such as a legislative body, department, bureau, board, or commission, and any further division. The title of the document underlined is given after the issuing agency. Commas are used between parts of the issuing agency and before the title.

The remainder of the information varies according to the document. It may include series, volume number, report number, or document number. If a publication has an author or editor, the name is given following the title. Congressional documents include the number of the Congress and the number of the session. If the publisher is the same as the issuing agency, it is omitted in the facts of publication. Both place and publisher are omitted in a serial type publication, such as the *Congressional Record* and *Parliamentary Debates*.

The following examples illustrate footnote citations of federal, state, and local documents, and of publications of the governments of other countries, and of international organizations.

a. United States

(1) Federal

[78]U.S., Congress, Senate, Committee on the Judiciary, Communism in Labor Unions, Hearings, 83d Cong., 2d Sess. (Washington, D.C.: Government Printing Office, 1954), p. 40.

[79]U.S., Congress, Senate, Congressional Record, 90th Cong., 1st Sess., 1967, 113, pt. 27, p. 36180.

[80]U.S., President, Economic Report of the President, Transmitted to the Congress, January 1967, together with the Annual Report of the Council of Economic Advisers (Washington, D.C.: Government Printing Office, 1967), p. 23.

[81]U.S., Bureau of the Census, The Population of Communist China: 1953, International Population Reports, Series P-90, no. 6, March 4, 1955 (Washington, D.C.: Government Printing Office, 1955), p. 3.

[82]U.S., Department of State, United States Relations with China, Far Eastern Series 30, Pub. 3573 (Washington, D.C.: Government Printing Office, 1949), pp. 127-136.

[83]U.S., Social Security Administration, Office of Research and Statistics, Sweden's Social Security System: An Appraisal of Its Economic Impact in the Postwar Period, by Carl G. Uhr, Research Report no. 14 (Washington, D.C.: Government Printing Office, 1966), p. 148.

A government publication with a personal author may be cited under the agency, as in the preceding example, or under the author's name, as in the folllowing example.

[83]Carl G. Uhr, Sweden's Social Security System: An Appraisal of Its Economic Impact in the Postwar Period, U.S., Social Security Administration, Office of Research and Statistics, Research Report no. 14 (Washington, D.C.: Government Printing Office, 1966), p. 148.

(2) State

[84]Nevada, Legislature, Handbook of the Nevada Legislature, Fifty-Third Session, 1965 (Carson City: State Printing Office, 1965), p. 10.

[85]Illinois, Secretary of State, Illinois Blue Book (Springfield, 1967), p. 105.

[86]California, State Department of Employment, <u>A Sourcebook on Unemployment Insurance in California</u> (Sacramento, 1953), p. 282.

(3) Local

[87]Los Angeles County, California, Office of the Superintendent of Schools, <u>Racial and Ethnic Survey</u> (Los Angeles, 1966), p. 98.

[88]Detroit, Rapid Transit Commission, <u>Plan for Modern Rapid Transit for Metropolitan Detroit, with a Suggested Plan for Financing Expressways and Rapid Transit</u> (Detroit, 1949), p. 99.

b. Other countries

[89]Great Britain, Parliament, <u>Parliamentary Debates</u> (House of Commons), ser. 5, vol. 765, no. 121 (May 20, 1968), pp. 2–3.

[90]Great Britain, Public Record Office, <u>Calendar of State Papers, Colonial Series, America and West Indies</u>, vol. 41, 1734–1735 (London: H. M. Stationery Office, 1953), p. 105.

[91]Great Britain, Colonial Office, Advisory Committee on Education in the Colonies, <u>Education for Citizenship in Africa</u>, Colonial No. 216 (London: H. M. Stationery Office, 1948), p. 21.

[92]Great Britain, Central Statistical Office, <u>Annual Abstract of Statistics</u>, no. 103 (London: H. M. Stationery Office, 1966), p. 202.

[93]France, Institut national de la statistique et des études économiques, <u>Code officiel géographique</u>, 3ᵉ éd. (Paris: Imprimerie nationale, 1961), p. 293.

[94]India, Ministry of Community Development, <u>Revision in the Programme of Community Development</u> (New Delhi: Government of India Press, 1958), p. 15.

[95]Canada, National Museum, <u>The Indians of Canada</u>, by Diamond Jenness, National Museum of Canada, Bulletin 65, Anthropological Series, 15 (Ottawa: Queen's Printer, 1960), p. 10.

c. International agencies

[96]United Nations, Secretariat, <u>The United Nations and Disarmament, 1945–1965</u> (Pub. 67.1.8) (New York, 1967), p. 212.

[97]United Nations, Economic and Social Council, Economic Commission for Africa, <u>Technical Assistance in Community Development and Related Fields</u> (E/CN.14/AC.1/2) (New York, 1959), p. 3.

[98]United Nations, Statistical Office, <u>The Growth of World Industry, 1938–1961: National Tables</u> (ST/STAT/Ser.P/2) (New York, 1963), p. 35.

[99]United Nations Educational, Scientific and Cultural Organization, <u>World Communication, Press, Radio, Television, Film</u>, 4th ed. (New York, 1964), p. 181.

[100]League of Nations, <u>Balances of Payments, 1939–1945</u> (Geneva, 1948), p. 178.

[101]North Atlantic Treaty Organization, <u>Atlantic Alliance: The Story of NATO</u> (Paris, 1953), p. 11.

[102]Organization for European Economic Cooperation, <u>The Organization for European Economic Cooperation: History and Structure</u>, 7th ed. (Paris, 1958), p. 52.

17. *Legal citations*

Special forms of citation are used in the field of law. They differ from the standard forms used in the humanities and social sciences fields in capitalization, punctuation, order of items, form of an author's name, facts of publication, abbreviations, and underlining of titles. A guide for this field is *A Uniform System of Citation*, 11th ed. (Cambridge, Mass.: Harvard Law Review Association, 1968). In papers predominantly on legal subjects, this guide should be followed. In papers in other fields, the style for citing books and periodicals in the field of law should conform to the style of other references in the paper. There are, however, special forms for citing court cases, constitutions, and laws. The complexities of these citations are explained in detail by the above mentioned guide. The sample footnotes below illustrate the forms used.

a. Court cases

Court cases are cited by the names of the parties, volume and page of the reporter, and date (year of decision). The court which decided the case is also included if it is not clear from the citation. If the name of the jurisdiction only is given, it is assumed that the court is the highest in the jurisdiction. Thus in footnote 103 the court is the U.S. Supreme Court.

[103]Peters v. Hobby, 349 U.S. 311 (1955).

The first ninety volumes of the United States Supreme Court Reports, up to 1875, are cited by the names of the reporters, as Howard, abbreviated to *How. U.S.* is added in the following citation since the court is not otherwise indicated.

[104]Luther v. Borden, 7 How. 1 (U.S. 1848).

In the following example N.Y.S. 2d indicates New York Supplement, Second Series.

[105]Parolisi v. Board of Examiners of City of New York, 285 N.Y.S. 2d 936 (1967).

The following example is a parallel citation of a state and a regional reporter.

[106]Bower v. Industrial Commission, 61 Ohio App. 469, 22 N.E. 2d 840 (1939).

b. Constitutions

Constitutions are cited by article (or amendment), section, and clause, if given. The date of the United States Constitution is not included. The date of a state constitution is included only if the constitution is no longer in force. Roman numerals are used for section numbers of the United States Constitution. Arabic numerals are used for section numbers of state constitutions.

[107]U.S. Const. art. I, sec. 8, cl. 8.

[108]U.S. Const. amend. XXII, sec. 1.

[109]Ill. Const. art. 4, sec. 3.

[110]N.Y. Const. art. 2, sec. 1 (1894).

c. Statutes

(1) Federal

In citing a federal law, the original statute and the citation to the *United States Code* are included. The *Statutes at Large* are cited by title (if any), volume, page, and date of enactment. References to the *United States Code* are made by title, section or sections, and date of the edition.

[111]Federal Food, Drug, and Cosmetic Act, 52 Stat. 1040 (1938), 21 U. S. C. sec. 301–392 (1958).

If the title has been mentioned in the text, the citation is as follows:

[111]52 Stat. 1040 (1938), 21 U. S. C. sec. 301–392 (1958).

Code titles which have been enacted into positive law (titles 1, 3, 4, 6, 9, 14, 17, 18, 28, 35) repeal the *Statutes at Large* from which they were derived. Therefore the original statute is not included in citations of these particular titles.

[112]Federal Youth Commission Act, 18 U. S. C. sec. 5005–5026 (1958).

In the following example the title is omitted because it has been mentioned in the text. The reference is to one specific section.

[113]18 U. S. C. sec. 5010 (1958).

(2) State

In citations of state laws, the date is given after the title. References are to chapters or sections.

114N.Y. Laws 1947, c. 17.

115Ill. Rev. Stat. 1949, c. 38.

116Utah Code Ann. 1943, sec. 21.

(3) Great Britain

English laws are cited by title, regnal year, name of sovereign (abbreviated), chapter, and section.

117Criminal Justice Act, 1948, 12 & 13 Geo. 6, c. 58, s. 38.

18. Unpublished materials

Unpublished materials include theses, dissertations, manuscripts, mimeographed reports, unpublished papers, letters, interviews, and television and radio programs. Titles of unpublished materials are enclosed in quotation marks. Otherwise the form of citation varies according to the type of material.

a. Thesis or dissertation

118Maria S. Young, "A Thematic Approach to Fiction" (Master's thesis, Drake University, 1967), p. 10.

119Frank Q. Sessions, "The Relationship between Geographical Mobility and Social Participation in a Stable Community" (Ph.D. dissertation, University of Utah, 1963), p. 85.

b. Manuscript

120"Horae Beatae Mariae," Library of Congress, Washington, D.C., Rosenwald Collection, MS No. 29.

c. Mimeographed report

121Joseph H. Zasloff, "Rural Resettlement in Viet Nam: An Agroville in Development" (Pittsburgh: University of Pittsburgh, August 6, 1962), p. 60. (Mimeographed.)

d. Unpublished paper

122John F. Goins, "Insults and the Law" (paper presented at the fifty-eighth annual meeting of the American Anthropological Association, Mexico City, Dec. 28, 1959), p. 2.

e. Letter

123Letter from Thomas Hart Benton to John Charles Frémont, June 22, 1847, Southwest Museum Library, Los Angeles, Calif., John Charles Frémont Papers.

f. Interview

    124Interview with Dr. Louis S. B. Leakey, Los Angeles,
Calif., March 27, 1963.

g. Television or radio program

    125"First Americans," NBC News Special, telecast, March 21,
1969. Narrated by Hugh Downs. Written and produced by Craig
Fisher.

19. *Shortened footnote citations*

    After the first complete footnote reference to a publication, later citations should be
in a shortened form.
    The Latin word *ibidem*, meaning "in the same place," abbreviated to *ibid.* is used
to refer to the work cited in the footnote immediately preceding. *Ibid.* is substituted for
as much of the preceding reference as is identical, and is followed by the new items such
as volume and page. If the reference is to the same volume and page of the work, *ibid.*
alone is used. Neither the author's name nor the title of the work should be used with
ibid. If the preceding footnote contains more than one reference, *ibid.* should not be used.

    1Morgan Kavanagh, <u>Origin of Language and Myths</u> (London:
S. Low, Son, and Marston, 1871), I, 164.

    2<u>Ibid</u>.

    3<u>Ibid</u>., II, 209.

    4George Knox, "Communication and Communion in Melville,"
<u>Renascence</u>, IX (Autumn, 1956), 27.

    5<u>Ibid</u>., p. 30.

    The use of *op. cit.* and *loc. cit.* is traditional practice in scholarly papers. *Op. cit.*,
for *opere citato*, meaning "in the work cited," is used with the author's surname when
repeated references to a work occur with interruptions by other footnotes. It is followed
by a specific page reference. *Loc. cit.*, for *loco citato*, meaning "in the place cited," is used
with the author's surname when the repeated reference is to the exact page previously
cited.

    1Isaac Goldberg, <u>The Wonder of Words</u> (New York: Frederick
Ungar, 1938), p. 386.

    2Siegfried H. Muller, <u>The World's Living Languages</u> (New
York: Frederick Ungar, 1964), p. 22.

    3Goldberg, <u>op. cit</u>., p. 408.

    4Muller, <u>loc. cit</u>.

In modern practice, however, the use of the author's surname and page, or the author's surname, title, and page is preferred to *op. cit.* and *loc. cit.* Footnotes 3 and 4 above could be given as:

3Goldberg, p. 408.

4Muller, p. 22.

or

3Goldberg, Wonder of Words, p. 408.

4Muller, World's Living Languages, p. 22.

The form giving the title after the author's name is recommended to prevent confusion, especially if there are references to more than one title by the same author, a number of intervening references after the first reference to a work, or several pages separating the references to a work.

If this style is used for later citations, it is permissible to give titles in shortened form. The shortened title should include the key words, not necessarily the first words, of the full title.

Full title:

American Democracy in Theory and Practice

Shortened form:

American Democracy

Full title:

An Essay toward an Indian Bibliography

Shortened form:

Indian Bibliography

B. BIBLIOGRAPHY

The bibliography is a list of sources used in the preparation of the paper. The bibliography differs from footnotes in form and in purpose. The principal differences in form are in indention, order of the author's name, and punctuation. The bibliography lists complete works whereas footnotes cite a specific page or pages.

Most bibliographies are only a listing of works. Some bibliographies are annotated. Annotations are brief descriptive notes. If annotations are given, they are typed one double space below the last line of the entry, indented ten spaces from the margin, single-spaced, in block form. See pages 123–139 for form. Some bibliographies are in the form of a bibliographical essay in which the references are included in running comment. In a bibliographical essay, full bibliographical information must be given for each reference, but the references need not be alphabetically arranged.

1. Placement

The bibliography is placed at the end of the paper. If there are appendixes, the bibliography may either precede or follow them. In books, bibliographies are sometimes placed at the end of each chapter. This is not recommended for research papers.

2. Arrangement

Bibliographies are usually in one alphabetical list according to the first word of the entry. Long bibliographies may be divided into sections according to types of material such as books and articles, or primary and secondary sources, or books by and about a writer if the paper is a study of one person. Entries are arranged alphabetically within each section.

3. Indention

Hanging indention is used for references in the bibliography. The author's name is placed flush with the left margin, and succeeding lines are indented five spaces from the margin.

4. Spacing

Single-spacing is used within items and double-spacing between items in the bibliography.

5. Capitalization

The rules for capitalization of titles of books, articles, and other works, given on page 51 should be followed in the bibliography.

6. Punctuation

The punctuation of entries in the bibliography differs from that of footnotes in that periods instead of commas are used to separate the major parts of the reference, and parentheses are not used to enclose the facts of publication for books. Detailed instructions for punctuation are given below in the discussion of various types of entries.

7. Books

Items included in entries for books are:

a. Author's full name
b. Title, including subtitle, if any
c. Editor, translator, illustrator, author of preface, if any
d. Series and number, if any
e. Volume number, if applicable
f. Edition, if other than the first
g. Facts of publication (place, publisher, date)

a. Author

In entries in a bibliography, the surname of the author is given first, followed by a comma and the given names or initials. A period is used after the name. See page 52 for the use of initials. If *Jr.* or a numeral follows a name, indicating that two or more persons in a family have identical names, this indication follows the given names or initials when the name is inverted (Jones, John J., Jr.; or Smith, James E. III). If there is more than one author, only the name of the first author needs to be inverted.

(1) One author

Nisbet, Robert A.   The Sociological Tradition.   New York:
    Basic Books, 1966.

(2) Two authors

If there are two authors, a comma is used following the given name or initial of the first author, and a period after the second author's name.

Easterbrook, W. T., and Hugh G. J. Aitken.   Canadian Economic
    History.   Toronto: Macmillan Company of Canada, 1956.

(3) Three authors

If there are three authors, a comma is used after the names of the first and second authors and a period after the third.

Sheats, Paul H., Clarence B. Jayne, and Ralph B. Spence.
    Adult Education: The Community Approach.   New York:
    Dryden Press, 1953.

(4) Four or more authors

If there are four or more authors, the name of the first author only is used, followed by a comma and *et al.* or *and others.*

Carr, Robert K., et al.   American Democracy in Theory and
    Practice.   3d ed.   New York: Holt, Rinehart and
    Winston, 1960.

(5) Two or more entries by the same author

If there is a successive listing of two or more entries by the same author, an unbroken line eight spaces in length, followed by a period, may be substituted for the author's name in the second and subsequent entries. A work by the same author with a coauthor is listed after the works by the author alone.

Randall, James G.   Constitutional Problems Under Lincoln.
    Rev. ed.   Urbana: University of Illinois Press, 1951.

_____.   Lincoln and the South.   Baton Rouge: Louisiana
    State University Press, 1946.

_____, and David Donald.   The Civil War and Reconstruction.
    2d ed.   Boston: D. C. Heath and Company, 1961.

(6) Pseudonymous author

The use of pseudonyms and real names in references is explained on page 52. The following examples illustrate the form for entries in the bibliography.

Porter, William S. [O. Henry]. <u>Sixes and Sevens</u>. Garden
    City, N.Y.: Doubleday, Page & Company, 1920.

Eliot, George [Marian Evans]. <u>Middlemarch</u>. London: Zodiac
    Press, 1950.

Caldwell, Taylor [pseud.]. <u>The Arm and the Darkness</u>. New
    York: Charles Scribner's Sons, 1943.

(7) Anonymous work

A work which has no known author is entered and alphabetized by the title.

<u>Song of Roland</u>. Translated by Leonard Bacon. New Haven,
    Conn.: Yale University Press, 1914.

If there is no author's name on the title page, but the author is known, his name is given in brackets.

[Prest, Thomas P.]. <u>The Smuggler King or the Foundling of
    the Wreck: A Nautico Domestic Romance</u>. London:
    E. Lloyd, 1844.

(8) Editor or compiler as author

If a book has an editor or compiler in place of an author, the given name or initial is followed by *ed.* or *comp.* separated from the name by a comma.

Wheelwright, Philip E., ed. <u>The Presocratics</u>. New York:
    Odyssey Press, 1966.

Mezirow, Jack D., and Dorothea Berry, comps. <u>The Literature
    of Liberal Adult Education, 1945-1957</u>. New York:
    Scarecrow Press, 1960.

(9) Society, association, or institution as author

American Sociological Association. <u>Directory, Constitution
    and By-Laws</u>. Washington, D.C.: American Sociological
    Association, 1967.

b. Title

As illustrated in the examples in Section a. above, the title is followed by a period in entries in the bibliography. Otherwise the form of the title is the same as in footnotes. The title should be given as it appears on the title page of the book. If there is punctuation within the title as it appears on the title page, this punctuation should be followed. If a book has a subtitle, it should be included and separated from the main part of the title by a colon. Capitalization should be according to the rules on page 51. The complete title is underlined. It is permissible to omit part of an unusually long title and indicate the omission by three spaced periods. A title within a title is enclosed in quotation marks. See examples on pages 53–54 for forms for a subtitle, a long title, and a title within a title.

c. Editor, translator, illustrator, author of preface

If a work has both an author and an editor, it is entered under the author's name and the editor's name follows the title. The same form is used for a translator or illustrator. Note in the examples below that *Edited*, *Translated*, and *Illustrated* are capitalized and spelled out. In footnote form they are in lowercase and abbreviated.

Wordsworth, William. <u>Literary Criticism</u>. Edited by Paul
    M. Zall. Lincoln: University of Nebraska Press, 1966.

Racine, Jean Baptiste. <u>Phaedra</u>. Translated by John Cairncross.
    Geneva: Librairie E. Droz, 1958.

Arnott, Kathleen. <u>African Myths and Legends</u>. Illustrated
    by Joan Kiddell—Monroe. New York: H. Z. Walck, 1963.

If the title page indicates that the book contains a preface or introduction by a well-known person, that information is included as illustrated in the following example.

Dunbar, Paul Laurence. <u>Lyrics of Lowly Life</u>. With an
    introduction by W. D. Howells. New York: Dodd, Mead
    and Company, 1906.

d. Series

If a book is part of a series, the title of the series is given following the title of the book. The series title, with the volume or publication number, if it has any, is followed by a period. A comma is used between the series title and the volume or publication number.

Von Laue, Theodore H. <u>Leopold Ranke: The Formative Years</u>.
    Princeton Studies in History, vol. 4. Princeton, N.J.:
    Princeton University Press, 1950.

Kroeber, Alfred L. <u>The Seri</u>. Southwest Museum Papers, no. 6.
    Los Angeles: Southwest Museum, 1931.

Spier, Leslie. <u>Plains Indian Parfleche Designs</u>. University
    of Washington Publications in Anthropology, vol. 4,
    no. 3. Seattle: University of Washington Press, 1931.

Hine, Robert V. <u>Edward Kern and American Expansion</u>. Yale
    Western Americana Series, 1. New Haven, Conn.: Yale
    University Press, 1962.

Davies, John G. <u>Early Christian Church</u>. History of Religion
    Series, edited by E. O. James. New York: Holt,
    Rinehart and Winston, 1965.

If there is an editor of the series, as in the preceding example, the name is given after the series title and is separated from it by a comma.

e. Edition

If the edition of a book is other than the first, this is indicated, usually by number, after the title. If the title page indicates the edition as *revised* but gives no number, the abbreviation *Rev. ed.* is used. If a number is given plus the words *revised* or *enlarged*, this information is given in abbreviated form. If the title page indicates that a person other than the author has been responsible for the revision, his name also is included.

Weaver, John C., and Fred E. Lukermann. World Resource
  Statistics. 2d ed. Minneapolis: Burgess Publishing
  Co., 1953.

Coman, Edwin T., Jr. Sources of Business Information.
  Rev. ed. Berkeley and Los Angeles: University of
  California Press, 1964.

Collison, Robert L. Bibliographies, Subject and National:
  A Guide to Their Contents, Arrangement and Use. 2d ed.
  rev. and enl. New York: Hafner Publishing Co., 1963.

Fowler, Henry W. A Dictionary of Modern English Usage.
  2d ed. rev. by Sir Ernest Gowers. Oxford: At the
  Clarendon Press, 1965.

If a reprint edition is used, the place, publisher, and date of both the original and the reprint editions may be given. It is also permissible to give the date only of the original publication omitting place and publisher, and the complete facts of publication for the reprint edition; or to give place, publisher, and date of the original publication and the date only of the reprint edition. See example and explanation on pages 55–56 For a bibliography entry the author's name would, of course, be inverted, and the parentheses around the facts of publication and the page reference would be omitted.

f. Number of volumes

If a work is in more than one volume, the number of volumes, in arabic numerals, precedes the facts of publication.

Peaslee, Amos J. International Governmental Organizations:
  Constitutional Documents. 2d ed. rev. 2 vols. The
  Hague: Martinus Nijhoff, 1961.

Southey, Robert. Life and Correspondence of Robert Southey.
  Edited by Charles C. Southey. 6 vols. London:.
  Longman, Brown, Green, and Longmans, 1849–50.

g. Facts of publication

As illustrated in the examples in this section, the facts of publication in entries in the bibliography are not enclosed in parentheses as they are in footnote references. The place of publication is preceded by a period and the date of publication is followed by a period. A colon is used after the place of publication and a comma after the name of the publisher.

See pages 56–58 for discussion and illustration of special problems concerning the facts of publication such as two or more places of publication, inclusion and abbreviation of the names of states and countries, the form of names of foreign cities, variations in the form of publishers' names, omission of the publisher, two publishers, names of foreign publishers, date of publication, copyright date, and special punctuation with dates.

h. Paging

The total paging of books is usually not given in scholarly bibliographies in the humanities and social sciences fields. Some institutions or departments, however, may require that it be given. If it is included, it is given at the end of the reference, in arabic numerals, with the abbreviation *pp.* following the numerals.

Nisbet, Robert A.   The Sociological Tradition.   New York:
     Basic Books, 1966.   349 pp.

8. *Special types of books*

a. Multivolume works

(1) A multivolume work with one author and title

Bulley, Margaret H.   Art and Everyman: Basis for
     Appreciation.   2 vols.   London: B. T. Batsford, 1952.

(2) One volume from a multivolume work with one author and title for the complete work, and a separate title for each volume

Churchill, Sir Winston L. S.   The Second World War.   Vol. I:
     The Gathering Storm.   Boston: Houghton Mifflin Company,
     1948.

(3) One volume from a multivolume work with one title and editor for the complete work and a different author and title for each volume

Brooke, Tucker.   The Renaissance (1500–1660).   Vol. II of
     Literary History of England, edited by Albert C. Baugh.
     4 vols.   New York: Appleton–Century–Crofts, 1948.

b. Foreign works

Capitalization of titles in foreign languages should be according to the rules on page 51.

(1) German

Baumgart, Reinhard.   Das Ironische und die Ironie in den
     Werken Thomas Manns.   Munich: Carl Hanser Verlag, 1964.

(2) French

Lebèque, Raymond.   Ronsard, l'homme et l'oeuvre.   Paris:
     Hatier–Boivin, 1957.

(3) Italian

```
Viscardi, Antonio.  La Letteratura italiana dalle origini ai
     giorni nostri.  Milan:  Istituto Editoriale Cisalpino,
     1951.
```

(4) Spanish

```
Valbuena Prat, Angel.  Historia del teatro español.  Barcelona:
     Editorial Noguer, 1956.
```

(5) Russian and other languages in non-Latin alphabets

Titles of works in Russian and other languages in non-Latin alphabets are transliterated. If a title is long, or not easily translated, the English translation of the title is given in brackets, but not underlined, after the transliterated title.

```
Kirpotin, Valerii I.  Dostoevskii i Belinskii.  Moscow:
     Sovetskoi Pisatel, 1960.

Moscow.  Akademiia Obshchestvennykh Nauk.  Russkaia
     progressivnaia filosofskaia mysl dvadtsatogo veka
     [Russian progressive philosophical thought of the
     twentieth century].  Moscow:  VPSh, 1959.
```

9. Component parts of books

One part from a book which is made up of several parts or chapters is listed under the author of the part, followed by the title of the part in quotation marks. The word *In* precedes the title of the whole book. The title of the book is underlined. It is followed by the name of the editor of the book. After the facts of publication, the complete paging of the part is given. The numerals for the page numbers are preceded by the abbreviation *Pp.*

```
Persons, Stow.  "The Origins of the Gentry."  In Essays
     in History and Literature, edited by Robert H. Bremner.
     Columbus:  Ohio State University Press, 1966.  Pp. 83-119.
```

10. Encyclopedia articles

Items included in entries for encyclopedia articles are:

a. Author of the article
b. Title of the article, in quotation marks
c. Title of the encyclopedia, underlined
d. Date, if no edition number appears on the title page
e. Volume number, in capital roman numerals
f. Inclusive paging

Place and publisher are omitted. If an edition number is given, the year is omitted. The abbreviations *vol.* and *pp.* are not used.

(1) Article with an author

Dickie, George T. "Aesthetics." <u>Encyclopedia Americana</u>.
     1967. I, 234–38.

(2) Article with no author

"Maronites." <u>Collier's Encyclopedia</u>. 1968. XVI, 441–42.

(3) Article from an encyclopedia with an edition number

Bryce, James. "Justinian I." <u>Encyclopaedia Britannica</u>.
     11th ed. XV, 596–602.

11. *Articles in periodicals*

Items included in entries for articles in periodicals are:

a. Author of the article
b. Title of the article
c. Title of the periodical
d. Series, if any
e. Volume number
f. Issue number (usually optional)
g. Date
h. Inclusive paging

a. Author of the article

The surname of the author of the article is given first, followed by a comma and the given name or initials. A period is used after the name. See pages 76–77 for other details concerning authors' names in bibliography entries.

b. Title of the article

The title of the article is enclosed in quotation marks and is followed by a period.

c. Title of the periodical

The title of the periodical is underlined and is followed by a comma. Capitalization of article and periodical titles should be according to the rules on page 51. If there is no author's name with an article, the article is alphabetized in the bibliography by the title.

d. Series

If a periodical has been issued in more than one series, this is indicated following the title of the periodical by the number of the series, as *2d ser.* or *n.s.* for "new series" or *o.s.* for "old series."

e. Volume number

It is recommended that the volume number be given in roman numerals to make it easily distinguishable from page numbers. The abbreviation *vol.* is not used before the volume number in references to periodical articles. Volume numbers are not necessary in references to daily or weekly publications.

f. Issue number

The issue number, if included, follows the volume number and is separated from it by a comma. If the issue number is included, it is permissible to omit the month or season from the date. It is also permissible to include volume number, issue number, and complete date. See examples on page 64. One form should be used consistently.

g. Date

The date of the issue of the periodical is enclosed in parentheses, except in a citation which does not include a volume number. No mark of punctuation immediately precedes the first parenthesis. A comma follows the second parenthesis. The date usually consists of the month or season and the year. In references to weekly and daily publications, the day of the month is included and the month is abbreviated. If a reference includes an issue number in addition to a volume number, or if paging is consecutive throughout a volume, the date may consist of the year only.

h. Paging

Inclusive paging of a periodical article is given in the bibliography. The abbreviation *pp.* is not used in references to periodical articles except when no volume number is given.

The place of publication and name of the publisher are not included in references to periodical articles.

(1) Article with an author

McLellan, David S. "The North African in France." Yale
    Review, XLIX (Spring, 1955), 421–38.

(2) Article with no author

"ASEE–Ford Foundation Residencies Program." School and
    Society, XCVII (January, 1969), 10–11.

(3) Article from a periodical which has been published in more than one series

Rowland, Benjamin. "The World's Image in Indian Architec-
    ture." Asian Review, n.s. II (April, 1965), 5–15.

(4) Article from a weekly periodical

"Japan in Search of Japan." Newsweek, Nov. 25, 1968, pp. 52–54.

(5) Articles in foreign languages

Rimbach, Guenther C. "Illusionsperspektiven in der modernen
    Lyrik." Germanisch–Romanische Monatsschrift, XIV
    (Oktober, 1964), 371–384.

Dagen, Jean. "Pour une histoire de la pensée de Fontenelle."
    Revue d'histoire littéraire de la France, LXVI (Octobre–
    Décembre, 1966), 619–641.

Gonella, Guido. "Aspectos negativos del sincretismo y del
    pragmatismo políticos." Revista de estudios políticos,
    CLVI (Novembre–Diciembre, 1967), 5–12.

Gagliardi, Donato. "Cicerone e il neoterismo." Rivista di
    filologia e di istruzione classica, 3d ser., XCVI
    (1968), 269–287.

12. Book reviews

The form for references to book reviews is similar to the form for references to articles in periodicals. The name of the reviewer is given first. If the review has a title, it is enclosed in quotation marks. The words *Review of* precede the title of the book reviewed. The title of the book is underlined and followed by a comma, the word *by*, and the name of the author. The remainder of the reference is the same as for a periodical article.

Greene, Donald J. Review of Johnsonian and Other Essays
    and Reviews, by R. W. Chapman. Review of English
    Studies, n.s. V (July, 1954), 332.

Altschul, Frank. "Doubting Thomas Diplomacy." Review of
    Between War and Peace, by Herbert Feis. Saturday
    Review, Oct. 1, 1960, p. 21.

13. Newspaper articles

References to a specific article in a newspaper should include:

a. Author's name, if given
b. Title of the article
c. Title of the newspaper
d. City, if not part of the title of the newspaper
e. Date
f. Section, if applicable
g. Page or pages
h. Column number (optional)

Hechinger, Fred M. "Schools vs. Riots." New York Times,
    July 30, 1967, sec. 4, p. 7, col. 3.

"Medical Briefs Urge Expansion." Globe and Mail (Toronto),
    Aug. 28, 1965, p. 8.

If files of a newspaper for a period of time have been consulted and several references have been made in footnotes, the entry in the bibliography may consist only of the title of the newspaper and the inclusive dates of the files used.

St. Louis Post Dispatch, Jan. 1–Nov. 30, 1955.

14. *Pamphlets*

References to pamphlets are given in the same form as references to books. The forms illustrated on page 78 should be used for pamphlets published in series.

15. *Government publications*

Items included and the order of items in references to government publications are discussed in the first two paragraphs of the section on footnote form for government publications on page 67. The form used for bibliography entries differs from footnote form in (1) the use of periods instead of commas between the major parts of the reference, (2) the omission of parentheses around the facts of publication, and (3) the omission of page references.

The following examples illustrate bibliography entries for federal, state, and local documents, and for publications of the governments of other countries and of international organizations.

a. United States

(1) Federal

U.S. Congress. Senate. Committee on the Judiciary.
    <u>Communism in Labor Unions</u>. Hearings, 83d Cong., 2d
    Sess. Washington, D.C.: Government Printing Office,
    1954.

U.S. Congress. Senate. <u>Congressional Record</u>. 90th Cong.,
    1st Sess. 1967. 113, pt. 27.

The place and publisher are omitted in the preceding example because it is a serial type publication.

U.S. President. <u>Economic Report of the President, Trans-</u>
    <u>mitted to the Congress, January, 1967, together with</u>
    <u>the Annual Report of the Council of Economic Advisers</u>.
    Washington, D.C.: Government Printing Office, 1967.

U.S. Department of State. <u>United States Relations with</u>
    <u>China</u>. Far Eastern Series 30, Pub. 3573. Washington,
    D.C.: Government Printing Office, 1949.

A government publication with a personal author may be entered under the agency or under the author's name.

U.S. Social Security Administration. Office of Research and
    Statistics. <u>Sweden's Social Security System: An</u>
    <u>Appraisal of Its Economic Impact in the Postwar Period</u>,
    by Carl G. Uhr. Research Report no. 14. Washington,
    D.C.: Government Printing Office, 1966.

or

Uhr, Carl G. <u>Sweden's Social Security System: An Appraisal
    of Its Economic Impact in the Postwar Period</u>. U.S. So-
    cial Security Administration, Office of Research and
    Statistics, Research Report no. 14. Washington, D.C.:
    Government Printing Office, 1966.

(2) State

Nevada. Legislature. <u>Handbook of the Nevada Legislature</u>,
    <u>Fifty-Third Session, 1965</u>. Carson City: State
    Printing Office, 1965.

Illinois. Secretary of State. <u>Illinois Blue Book</u>.
    Springfield, 1967.

California. State Department of Employment. <u>A Sourcebook
    on Unemployment Insurance in California</u>. Sacramento, 1953.

(3) Local

Los Angeles County. California. Office of the Superintendent
    of Schools. <u>Racial and Ethnic Survey</u>. Los Angeles,
    1966.

Detroit. Rapid Transit Commission. <u>Plan for Modern Rapid
    Transit for Metropolitan Detroit, with a Suggested
    Plan for Financing Expressways and Rapid Transit</u>.
    Detroit, 1949.

b. Other countries

Great Britain. Parliament. <u>Parliamentary Debates</u> (House
    of Commons). Ser. 5, vol. 765, no. 121. May 20, 1968.

The place and publisher are omitted from the preceding example because it is a serial
type publication.

Great Britain. Public Record Office. <u>Calendar of State
    Papers, Colonial Series, America and West Indies</u>.
    Vol. 41, 1734–1735. London: H. M. Stationery Office,
    1953.

Great Britain. Colonial Office. Advisory Committee on
    Education in the Colonies. <u>Education for Citizenship
    in Africa</u>. Colonial No. 216. London: H. M. Stationery
    Office, 1966.

France. Institut national de la statistique et des études
    économiques. <u>Code officiel géographique</u>. 3e éd.
    Paris: Imprimerie nationale, 1961.

India. Ministry of Community Development. <u>Revision in the
    Programme of Community Development</u>. New Delhi: Govern-
    ment of India Press, 1938.

Canada. National Museum. The Indians of Canada, by Diamond
    Jenness. National Museum of Canada, Bulletin 65,
    Anthropological Series, 15. Ottawa: Queen's Printer,
    1960.

c. International organizations

United Nations. Economic and Social Council. Economic
    Commission for Africa. Technical Assistance in Community
    Development and Related Fields. E/CN.14/AC.1/2. New
    York, 1959.

United Nations Educational, Scientific and Cultural Organi-
    zation. World Communication, Press, Radio, Television,
    Film. 4th ed. New York, 1964.

League of Nations. Balances of Payments, 1939-1945. Geneva,
    1948.

North Atlantic Treaty Organization. Atlantic Alliance: The
    Story of NATO. Paris, 1953.

Organization for European Economic Cooperation. The Organi-
    zation for European Economic Cooperation: History and
    Structure. 7th ed. Paris, 1958.

16. *Unpublished materials*

The form of references to unpublished materials varies according to the type of
material. All titles of unpublished works are enclosed in quotation marks.

a. Thesis or dissertation

Young, Maria S. "A Thematic Approach to Fiction." Master's
    thesis, Drake University, 1967.

Sessions, Frank Q. "The Relationship between Geographical
    Mobility and Social Participation in a Stable Community."
    Ph.D. dissertation, University of Utah, 1963.

b. Mimeographed report

Zasloff, Joseph H. "Rural Resettlement in Viet Nam: An
    Agroville in Development." Pittsburgh: University
    of Pittsburgh, Aug. 6, 1962. Mimeographed.

c. Unpublished paper

Goins, John F. "Insults and the Law." Paper presented at the
    fifty-eighth annual meeting of the American Anthropological
    Association, Mexico City, Dec. 28, 1959.

d. Manuscript material

An entire manuscript collection is usually listed in a bibliography rather than individual items. The name of the city is given first, followed by the name of the depository and the name of the collection.

Los Angeles, Calif. Southwest Museum Library. John
    Charles Frémont papers.

If it is desirable to list an individual item, the number, if any, and title of the item are given at the end of the reference.

Washington, D.C. Library of Congress. Rosenwald Collection.
    MS No. 29. "Horae Beatae Mariae."

IV
Tables
and Illustrations

A. TABLES

Detailed statistical material may be presented in tables rather than in the text of the paper. Tables should be used to supplement but not to duplicate material in the text. Each table should present one subject or one kind of data rather than a complexity of ideas or comparisons of different kinds. Data should be organized with clearness and accuracy.

1. Placement

A table should appear as near as possible to the portion of the text in which it is discussed. If the table is short, it can be placed on the page with the text, immediately following the first mention of it. If there is not sufficient room for the table on the page on which it is mentioned, it should be placed on the next page at the end of the first paragraph. Tables inserted in the text should be separated from the text by three spaces above and below. See page 90 for a sample table on a page with text.

Large tables should be placed on a separate page with no text. See sample table on page 91. Wide tables should be placed broadside with the table number and caption at the binding edge of the page. See sample table on page 92. Tables too wide to be placed broadside may be placed on two opposite pages with the parts of the table the same dimension on both pages. See sample table on pages 94 and 95. Tables too wide to be handled in this manner may be reduced in size by a photographic process or folded. If folded, there should be one-half inch between the fold and the right edge of the manuscript so the table will not be cut in trimming for binding.

A table which is too long for one page, but not too wide, may be continued on the next page. The heading on the second page should consist of the word *Table* followed by the number and the word *continued* in parentheses on the same line as illustrated below. The heading is centered. The caption is not repeated.

TABLE 5 (continued)

Very long tables should be placed in an appendix rather than in the body of the paper.

Uptake of Iron by the Macadamia from Various Chelates

The basis of the change from use of FeHEDDHA to NaFeDTPA was a sand culture trial in which the leaf iron content of plants supplied with FeEDTA, FeHEDDHA, and NaFeDTPA was compared to a control to which no iron was added. Each treatment was replicated four times in a randomized block layout with one tree per pot, and two pots per plot, and the experiment was run for a period of twelve months commencing in January 1965. The pots were set on the automatic watering system previously described. Leaf samples were taken in January 1966, using three-month-old leaves (tagged to insure that this was their correct age), and these were analyzed for their iron content. Results are shown in Table 1.

TABLE 1.   Leaf iron content (ppm) of trees supplied with three different chelates as source of iron

Treatment	Replicate				Mean	Statistical Significance (5% level)
	1	2	3	4		
Control—no iron	11.2	14.6	10.6	11.2	11.9	a
FeEDTA	25.2	25.2	28.8	30.4	27.4	b
FeHEDDHA	46.8	35.3	41.2	32.5	28.9	c
NaFeDTPA	42.0	57.0	38.2	32.5	42.4	c

It is seen in Table 1 that FeEDTA is inferior to both FeHEDDHA and NaFeDTPA. This may be because, in the nutrient

TABLE 7

RATIOS OF ISOENZYMIC RIBOSEPHOSPHATE ISOMERASE
ACTIVITIES IN SPINACH LEAF FRACTIONS

Fraction	Volume* (ml)	Ribosephosphate Isomerase Isoenzymes (major/minor)
Cytoplasm	590	0.72 (489/694)†
Cytoplasm	100	0.56 (101/180)
Chloroplast Extract	48	4.3 (38.1/8.8)
Chloroplast Extract	100	117 (1520/13)
Chloroplast Extract	33	16.7 (68.6/4.1)

*The volume of the fraction is the volume
that was subfractionated.

†The numbers in parentheses are the actual
units of each isomerase isoenzyme obtained.

TABLE 1

DATA OBTAINED FROM DETERMINATIONS OF CO_2 PERCENT IN TANKS WITH COMPRESSED GASES

Avg. % CO_2	Barometric Pressure (mm Hg)	Temp. °C	Corrected* H_2O Vol. l	Wt CO_2 Absorbed† (gm)	Moles CO_2 Absorbed	Vol. CO_2 at stp (l)	Total Vol. of Gas (l)	% CO_2 (Vol.)
0.098	728.7	26	8.45	0.0164	0.000373	0.00835	8.5	0.098
	730.3	28	8.45	0.0164	0.000373	0.00835	8.5	0.098
0.384	731.4	26	8.45	0.0638	0.00145	0.0325	8.5	0.382
	731.3	27	8.45	0.0648	0.00147	0.0329	8.5	0.387
3.30	730.5	28	5.02	0.3380	0.00769	0.172	5.19	3.31
	728.6	29	4.98	0.3354	0.00762	0.170	5.15	3.30
42.6	727.7	28	1.678	2.4125	0.0548	1.228	2.906	42.26
	727.1	29	0.829	1.2235	0.0278	0.6227	1.4513	42.91

*Corrected to standard temperature, pressure, and for water vapor pressure.

†Weight of CO_2 absorbed on Ascarite.

2. Numbering

Arabic numerals are used for numbering tables. Tables should be numbered consecutively throughout the paper. The table number, followed by the caption, is placed above the table.

3. Captions

There are two commonly used styles of table captions. In one style, the word "Table" is typed in capital letters flush with the left edge of the table, and is followed by the number and a period. The caption is typed immediately following on the same line. If the caption is longer than one line, the first line is typed the width of the table and the second and succeeding lines are indented in inverted pyramid form. The lines are single-spaced. Lowercase letters are used except for the first letter of the first word and of proper nouns and proper adjectives. No end punctuation is used. One double-space is left between the caption and the top line of the table.

```
TABLE 3.  Analysis of variance on the effect of temperature,
       organic matter, and flooding time on the quantity
               of iron and manganese in solution


===================================================================
```

In the second style, the word "Table" in capital letters, followed by the number, is centered on a line by itself. The caption, also in capital letters, is centered on the second space below the table number, with no end punctuation. If the caption is longer than one line, the second and succeeding lines are indented in inverted pyramid form and single-spaced. One double-space is left between the caption and the top line of the table.

```
                        TABLE 4

          EFFECT OF GERMINATION AND ROOT LENGTH
               IN RELATION TO SALINITY OF
                  FIVE DIFFERENT SOILS


          =================================================
```

The same style for table captions should be used throughout the paper.

4. Columns

a. Headings

Within a table each column should have a heading centered above the items to which it applies, and centered between the horizontal lines above and below it. Column headings may be on two or more levels as illustrated by the sample table on page 90. In column headings the first and last words, and all nouns, pronouns, adverbs, adjectives, and verbs should be capitalized. These headings should be single-spaced if they are longer than one line. If the headings are too long to be placed in the normal position, they may be run upward either vertically or diagonally to the right as in the sample table on page 96.

TABLE 1. Amino acids, amides, and other constituents of the amino acid

Treat-ment	Mn	Fe	Ser	Gly	Ala	Val	Leu	Glu	Orn	Arg
	ppm	ppm								
Control	101.5	32.5	ND	6.20	17.70	3.62	0.40	33.00	0.67	172.25
	176.0	35.3	ND	9.75	23.05	4.05	0.37	42.00	1.40	107.25
	91.2	42.0	14.07	5.37	27.27	4.05	0.35	33.87	0.62	104.50
	149.0	57.0	25.12	10.95	31.75	4.67	0.55	38.25	0.95	118.00
	205.0	20.4	18.95	8.22	23.20	4.40	0.37	43.50	1.25	156.50
	179.0	23.0	ND	5.72	14.65	1.90	0.35	17.80	1.52	168.50
Average			19.37	7.70	22.93	3.82	0.40	34.73	1.07	137.82
Mn-def.	0.6	25.2	ND	7.90	16.75	3.45	0.80	16.12	1.22	113.75
	0.6	25.8	ND	14.52	23.12	7.77	1.20	23.00	1.00	117.75
	6.7	28.0	ND	12.90	18.90	3.40	0.80	39.30	1.95	151.50
	2.9	28.6	31.75	7.90	19.22	4.87	0.55	43.75	1.35	77.50
	2.9	28.0	28.50	14.65	22.50	6.55	0.35	38.50	2.35	63.50
	2.6	47.1	26.25	6.45	20.60	3.47	0.40	38.75	2.37	99.00
Average			28.83	10.72	20.18	4.91	0.68	33.23	1.70	103.83
Fe-def.	98.0	10.6	ND	11.40	33.75	5.55	0.62	44.25	3.35	317.50
	232.0	11.8	ND	9.02	16.30	4.80	0.57	33.40	2.17	452.50
	82.0	11.2	ND	15.35	30.00	4.87	0.57	20.22	8.12	245.50
	160.0	14.2	15.60	4.00	36.00	5.05	0.40	44.72	1.95	423.75
	190.0	16.1	34.37	8.40	17.25	5.55	0.42	38.25	1.62	292.50
	125.0	11.2	11.65	4.27	21.00	3.55	0.45	26.25	1.70	348.75
Average			20.54	8.74	25.71	4.89	0.50	34.52	3.15	346.75

*Et PO_4 = ethanolamine phosphate.

fraction in iron- and manganese-deficient macadamia leaves

γ-amino butyric	Asp	Homo	Lys	Thr	Lleu	His	Tyr	φala	Glu NH$_2$	Asp NH$_2$	Et PO$_4$*
7.05	23.40	2.87	20.90	5.42	0.70	6.75	3.67	2.35	ND	ND	3.10
9.15	27.50	6.60	26.50	7.60	0.82	6.45	5.10	1.10	ND	ND	3.75
3.70	23.95	3.47	18.55	4.00	1.17	2.45	0.37	0.27	28.25	32.50	4.70
6.92	31.00	3.35	19.12	4.82	1.45	3.65	0.52	0.47	30.75	39.50	4.82
3.67	23.45	2.97	24.35	4.95	0.87	6.85	1.72	0.87	24.37	30.50	4.32
9.10	17.10	3.52	16.30	3.35	0.95	3.85	6.75	0.30	ND	ND	2.92
6.59	24.40	3.80	20.95	5.02	0.99	5.00	1.99	0.89	27.79	34.13	3.92
1.65	12.98	2.35	7.95	3.50	0.97	1.52	1.42	0.30	ND	ND	4.57
3.72	26.02	9.25	13.92	12.27	3.35	2.27	3.00	0.82	ND	ND	4.40
6.27	29.75	9.80	41.95	5.42	1.00	7.27	5.15	1.30	ND	ND	3.35
2.80	28.75	4.55	15.75	6.25	1.32	2.72	0.75	0.37	37.25	28.25	5.05
2.75	25.22	3.90	6.97	6.10	1.45	4.47	0.95	0.45	10.60	13.25	2.75
5.90	27.25	11.32	10.00	5.37	1.57	3.85	0.62	0.35	29.00	18.50	4.22
3.84	24.99	6.86	16.09	6.48	1.61	3.68	1.98	0.59	25.61	20.00	4.05
6.60	37.50	13.07	42.75	7.65	1.10	4.97	2.57	0.22	ND	ND	3.90
8.47	40.87	12.27	35.50	8.67	1.12	4.82	4.52	0.25	ND	ND	4.57
4.07	20.60	9.55	25.37	7.00	2.30	4.80	4.05	1.22	ND	ND	2.82
5.40	37.50	8.60	43.52	5.60	3.57	4.35	2.70	0.95	30.50	20.50	3.55
11.60	39.25	6.50	33.42	6.67	2.40	7.70	0.60	0.30	23.75	58.50	3.44
2.30	21.17	9.40	28.00	3.35	0.70	4.90	1.85	1.05	29.00	13.40	4.85
6.40	32.81	9.90	34.76	6.49	1.86	5.25	2.71	0.67	27.75	30.80	3.85

TABLE 10

SURFACE FIELD AND LABORATORY DATA: RIVERSIDE AREA

Station	V_p Compressional Velocity, ft./sec.	V_s Shear Wave Velocity, ft./sec.	σ Poisson's Ratio	E_d Dynamic Elastic Modulus, psi $\times 10^3$	G_d Dynamic Shear Modulus, psi $\times 10^3$	ρ Bulk Density g/cm³	ρmax Maximum Density g/cm³	% Relative Density %	τ Shear Strength, psi
1	1050	400	.39	10.0	2.95	1.48	1.73	85.6	12.2
2	1200	400	.42	12.0	3.60	1.77	1.87	94.5	7.8
3	1200	400	.36	9.6	2.90	1.46	1.76	82.7	8.6
4	1180	350	.33	11.8	2.60	1.65	1.84	90.0	10.9
5	1200	320	.36	7.2	1.80	1.32	1.65	80.4	2.9
6	1300	400	.41	10.0	2.95	1.49	1.81	82.8	7.4
7	1100	440	.42	12.0	4.10	1.66	1.86	89.0	7.5
8	800	400	.33	11.0	3.50	1.71	1.84	91.0	3.5
9	1180	500	.37	17.0	5.20	1.62	1.80	89.8	8.2
10	1240	480	.40	14.0	4.50	1.50	1.76	84.7	12.1
11	1280	480	.36	15.0	4.50	1.51	1.85	81.8	8.2
12	1160	450	.41	11.0	3.60	1.37	1.62	84.5	7.6
13	1120	360	.44	8.0	2.40	1.46	1.59	91.6	7.6
14	1160	500	.32	16.0	5.00	1.57	1.84	85.5	8.6
15	1100	500	.33	16.0	4.90	1.51	1.79	84.6	0.6

TABLE 5. Radioactivity incorporated in the organic acid, amino acid, and lipid fractions of excised iron- and manganese-deficient macadamia leaves following different periods of Cl4 acetate feeding (cpm incorporated per gram fresh weight of leaf)

Feeding Period (Min.) (1)	Control Leaves			Mn-deficient Leaves			Fe-deficient Leaves		
	Amino Acid (2)	Org. Acid (3)	Lipid (4)	Amino Acid (5)	Org. Acid (6)	Lipid (7)	Amino Acid (8)	Org. Acid (9)	Lipid (10)
15	70	121	0	48	355	0	75	731	0
30	105	539	0	59	1509	0	158	3284	0
60	182	1355	0	120	3344	0	294	4913	0
120	204	1324	0	160	2685	0	362	5365	0
180	186	1021	0	192	2618	0	376	4633	0

b. Alignment

Columns of words are aligned on the left. Columns of numbers are aligned on the right unless there are decimals. If there are decimals, alignment is by the decimal points. See sample table on page 92 and other sample tables in this section.

c. Numbering

If a table consists of several columns and references to them are made in the text, it may be helpful to number them. Numbering should be from left to right with all columns numbered, including the stub (the first column on the left). The numerals are enclosed in parentheses and centered above or below all column headings depending upon which position is clearer in the particular table concerned. See sample table on page 97.

5. Ruling

Double horizontal lines should be placed at the top of a table, a single line below the column headings, and a single line at the bottom of the table. If a table consists of three or more columns, vertical lines may be used to separate the columns. See sample table on page 97. There should be one blank space on each side of these lines. It is permissible to omit vertical lines if the spacing of the material allows it to be read easily.

6. Footnotes

Explanatory footnotes are placed immediately below a table, with the first note beginning two spaces below the bottom line of the table. The first line of each footnote is indented five spaces from the left edge of the table. The second and succeeding lines are flush with the left edge of the table. Single-spacing is used within each footnote and double-spacing between footnotes.

These footnotes are indicated by superscript lowercase letters (a, b, c) or by symbols placed after the items in the table. The same letters or symbols precede the footnotes. If symbols are used, the sequence should be asterisk (*), dagger (†), double dagger (‡), section mark (§), and parallel (‖). If more are needed, these symbols may be doubled (**, ††, ‡‡, etc.)

If there is only one footnote to a table, an asterisk should be used in place of the letter *a*. If there are footnotes to various parts of a table such as column headings, stub, and items in the columns, the sequence of superscript letters or symbols should be from left to right, row by row, not from top to bottom by column.

See sample tables on pages 91, 92, and 94 for placement and form of footnotes.

7. Spacing and type

Spacing of material in the body of the table may be either single or double. Elite type may be preferable to pica for large tables.

For spacing between text and tables, spacing of captions, column headings, and footnotes, see the appropriate sections above.

8. Margins

The standard margins of $1\frac{1}{2}$ inches at the left, 1 inch at the right, and $1\frac{1}{4}$ inches at the top and bottom of the page should be observed for pages containing tables. It is permissible, however, to exceed the margins slightly, except on the left, in order to get a large table on one page. The $1\frac{1}{2}$ inch margin at the left must be observed because it is the binding edge. The other three margins should not be less than ½ inch because of trimming for binding.

9. Pagination

Pages containing tables are numbered consecutively with the other pages in the paper. The page number is placed in the normal position at the top of the page regardless of how the table is placed on the page.

10. References in the text

A reference made in the text to a table should be by table number if the reference is on the same or preceding page. On any other page the reference should be by both table number and page number.

```
Results of the study are presented in TABLE 2.
Information on adult longevity is presented in TABLE 12,
page 69.
```

B. ILLUSTRATIONS

Besides tables, other forms for presenting statistical material are graphs, charts, and statistical maps. Types of graphs commonly used are curve, bar, and circle, also called sector or pie. Nonstatistical material is presented in forms such as diagrams, organizational charts, drawings, photographs, and maps.

See pages 102–105 for examples of illustrations.

1. Placement

Illustrations generally should be placed as near as possible to the text containing the discussion of them. In some papers, however, it may be desirable to place all illustrations of one type at the end or in an appendix.

Small illustrations may be placed on pages with text. Large illustrations should be on separate pages. Wide illustrations may be placed broadside or on two opposite pages. The same rules that apply to the placement of tables apply also to the placement of illustrations. See page 89.

2. Numbering and labeling

If illustrations of several types are included, all except plates are labeled figures and numbered consecutively throughout the paper with arabic numerals. The word *Figure* or the abbreviation *Fig.*, followed by the numeral and legend, should be placed below the illustration.

If there are a number of illustrations of one type, they may be grouped together and labeled by specific name, such as maps, and numbered as a separate series.

Usually full-page illustrations, especially photographs, are labeled plates. Plates are numbered as a separate series with capital roman numerals. The heading *Plate*, in capital letters, followed by the numeral, is centered above the illustration. If a plate is composed of more than one illustration, each may be lettered (*A*, *B*, etc.) and each given a legend. The use of letters rather than numbers prevents confusion with the series of figure numbers. See form on page 100.

The legend or legends for a full-page illustration should be placed on the facing page.

PLATE I

A

B

This arrangement should be used for any illustration which is too large to allow sufficient room for the legend within the standard margins.

3. Legends

The title of an illustration is usually called a legend rather than a caption. A legend may be placed on the line with *Figure* or *Fig.*, followed by the number and a period, on the second space below the illustration. If this style is used, the legend is typed in lowercase letters except for the first letter of the first word and of proper nouns and proper adjectives. If the legend is short, it is centered. If it is longer than one line, the first line is indented five spaces from the left margin and the second and subsequent lines are flush with the margin. The legend is single-spaced if longer than one line. It is punctuated with a period at the end.

```
     Figure 2.  Water desorption curves for soils used in
germination studies.
```

In another style, the word *Figure* in capital letters, with the number following, is placed on a line by itself on the second space below the illustration. The legend is in capital letters and is centered two spaces below the figure number. If it is longer than one line, it should be indented in inverted pyramid form and single-spaced.

FIGURE 2

WATER DESORPTION CURVES FOR SOILS
USED IN GERMINATION STUDIES

The same style should be used for all legends in the paper.

4. Hand-drawn illustrations

Hand-drawn illustrations should be done in india ink and duplicated by a photographic process for additional copies. It is not advisable to use colors if the illustrations are to be photographically reproduced or if the entire paper, thesis, or dissertation is to be reproduced in microfilm or xerographic form. Lettering may be done by typewriter or in india ink.

Special manuals on graphic presentation may be consulted for details on types, planning, construction, and reproduction. Recommended are: Calvin F. Schmid, *Handbook of Graphic Presentation* (New York: Ronald Press, 1954); Anna C. Rogers, *Graphic Charts Handbook* (Washington, D.C.: Public Affairs Press, 1961); Charles S. Papp, *Making Graphs and Maps* (Dubuque, Iowa: W. C. Brown, 1968); and Charles S. Papp, *Scientific Illustration, Theory and Practice* (Dubuque, Iowa: W. C. Brown, 1968).

5. Oversized illustrations

Oversized illustrations should generally be reduced to standard page size by a photographic process. If reduction in size is not desirable for some illustrations, they may be folded to be bound into the manuscript. If they are folded, the outer fold should be at least ½ inch from the right edge of the page so that it will not be cut in trimming for binding. If there is also a fold at the left side, it should be 1½ inches from the left edge of the page so that it will not be stitched in binding.

Material too large to be folded and bound into the manuscript may be folded to a maximum size of 8 x 10 inches to be inserted into a pocket which will be placed on the inside back cover when the manuscript is bound.

6. Reproduction of illustrations

The student should determine whether reproduction of original illustrations by a process such as xerography is acceptable for additional copies of a thesis or dissertation, or whether original illustrations are required for all official copies in his institution.

Reproductions in black and white of illustrations in which color has been used are usually not satisfactory.

7. Paper

Paper used for illustrations should be white opaque paper of 16- or 20-pound weight, the same weight as that used for the text. If special paper is used for some types of illustrations, it should be as nearly the same weight as possible.

8. Mounting

Illustrative material smaller than standard page size may be mounted on typing paper with dry mounting tissue or plastic glue. Rubber cement, Scotch tape, mucilage, photo-corners, paper clips, and staples should not be used. Standard margins should be observed in mounting material, and room should be allowed for the legend if it is to appear on the page with the illustration. Some institutions do not accept mounted material in theses and dissertations and require that pages with mounted material be photographed.

9. Margins

Pages containing illustrations should have the standard margins of $1\frac{1}{2}$ inches on the left, 1 inch on the right, and $1\frac{1}{4}$ inches at top and bottom. These margins may be exceeded slightly, except on the left, if it is necessary in order to place a large illustration on one page. Facing pages should have the $1\frac{1}{2}$ inch margin on the right which is the binding edge for these pages.

10. Pagination

All full-page illustrations and facing pages containing legends should be numbered consecutively with the other pages of the text. The page numbers should be in the normal position regardless of the position of the illustration on the page.

11. Footnotes

If explanatory footnotes are used for illustrations, they should be placed two spaces below the legend. Otherwise the same rules that apply to footnotes to tables should be followed. Inclusion of explanatory material in the legend or in the text is generally preferable to the use of footnotes for illustrations.

12. References in the text

A reference in the text to a figure or plate should be by figure or plate number if the reference is on the same page or the preceding page. On any other page the reference should be by both figure or plate number and page number.

(Sample curve graph)

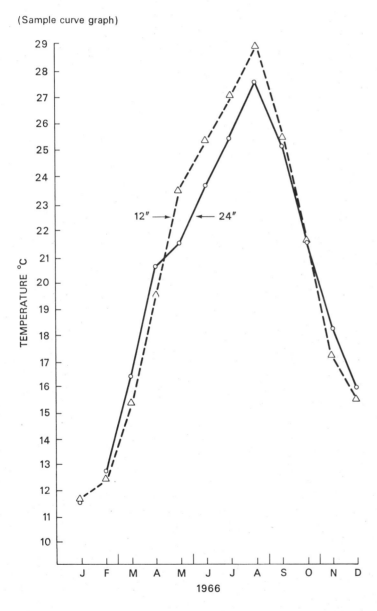

Fig. 6. Soil temperatures during 1966
at 12– and 24–inch depths in a citrus
orchard near Mecca, California.

(Sample bar graph)

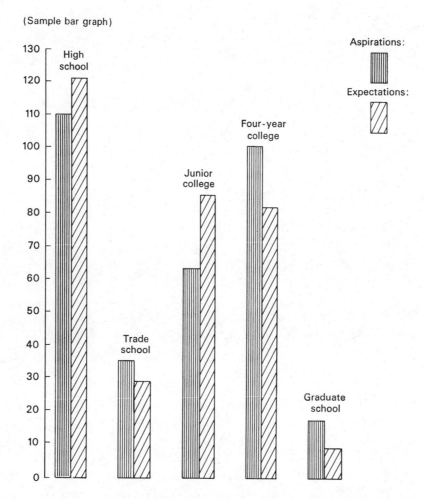

Figure 17. Comparison of Mexican–American public school students' educational aspirations and educational expectations, Los Angeles, 1966.

(Sample circle, sector, or pie graph)

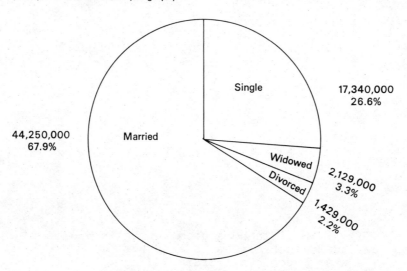

Figure 10. Marital status of the male population of the United States, 1965.
Statistics are from the <u>Statistical Abstract</u> <u>of the United States</u>, 1966.

(Sample diagram)

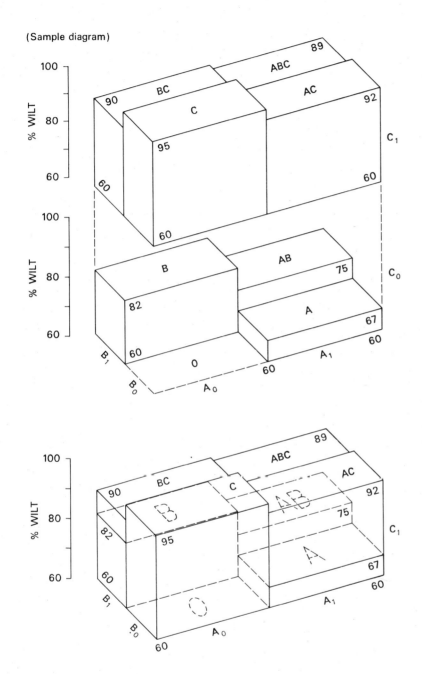

Figure 9. Three-dimensional relationship of the pathogenicity of three isolate (A-204, B-207, C-211) and combinations of F. oxysporum f. lini on three diploid and tetraploid flax varieties: Imperial, Abyssinian Yellow, Imperial x Q0407.

(Sample administrative organizational chart)

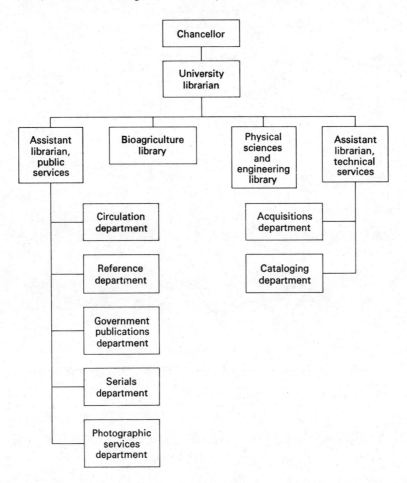

V
Scientific Papers

The writing of scientific papers is treated in a separate section because of the differences between the scientific fields and other academic fields in regard to the physical format of research papers.

It is difficult to formulate general rules for scientific papers because of variations in practice from field to field, and even within fields of specialization. This section presents general practices which apply to all scientific fields in the organization of the paper and the handling of references to literature, and illustrates the specific practices of individual fields.

A. ORGANIZATION

Usually in a scientific paper, an abstract or summary is given before the beginning of the text. This is followed by an introduction stating the nature of the problem, purpose, scope, method of investigation, and results of the investigation; a description of materials and methods used; a description of experiments; and results and conclusions.

A short paper is typed continuously. In a longer paper, each major section begins on a new page, with sections either numbered or titled or both. Subheadings are given within major sections but do not begin on new pages.

Arrangement and description of the parts of a thesis or dissertation, discussed on pages 27–47, apply to scientific as well as other academic fields. Suggestions for the presentation of illustrations and tables, pages 89–105, and for typing the manuscript, pages 117–120, apply to scientific papers.

B. DOCUMENTATION

1. List of references

In theses and dissertations in all scientific fields, references to literature are given at the end in a list with the heading *References, References Cited,* or *Literature Cited.* Placement of references at the end of articles is also followed by many journals. The references may be arranged alphabetically by authors or in the order of appearance in the text and numbered.

If the list is arranged alphabetically by authors, references are arranged chronologically under each author. If there is more than one work by the same author in the same year, lowercase letters *a, b, c* are added to the date.

(1960a, 1960b)

2. *References in the text*

a. References by author and date

If the alphabetical arrangement is used, references in the text are made by giving the name of the author with the date of publication immediately following in parentheses on the line. Square brackets should be used for the sake of clarity if other series of numbers have been placed in parentheses in the text.

To facilitate modal analyses, K-feldspars of the slabbed rocks were stained yellow by the method of Chayes (1956)

The reference is to:

Chayes, F., 1956, Petrographic modal analysis: New York, J. Wiley, 113 p.

b. References by author and number

If the list is arranged in the order of appearance in the text, the references are numbered consecutively. References in the text are made by giving the name of the author followed by the number of the reference placed in parentheses or square brackets on the line.

Examples of the first category are according to Leopold (21)

The reference is to:

21. Leopold, A. C. 1964. Plant growth and development. McGraw-Hill, New York. 395 p.

A numbered list may be alphabetized as well as numbered, with references in the text made by author and number as in the second example above. The numbers will not be in consecutive order in the text if this method is used.

c. Author's name in parentheses

If the author's name does not occur in the sentence in the text, the name is also enclosed in parentheses.

Nonparametric tests were used for all comparisons (Siegel, 1956).

The reference is to:

Siegel, S. <u>Nonparametric statistics for the behavioral</u>
     <u>sciences</u>. New York: McGraw–Hill, 1956.

d. References with two or more authors

Any reference to a work by two authors should give both names.

Cohen and Adams (1966) or Cohen and Adams (2)

The first reference to a work by three authors should give all three names, but subsequent references to the same work should give the name of the first author only, followed by *et al.*, meaning "and others."

First reference

Pitts, Sharp, and Chan (1964)

or

Pitts, Sharp, and Chan (38)

Subsequent references

Pitts <u>et al</u>. (1964) or Pitts <u>et al</u>. (38)

For works by four or more authors, the name of the first author only, followed by *et al.*, is used for all references including the first.

Sawyer <u>et al</u>. (1959) or Sawyer <u>et al</u>. (45)

e. References by number only

A third type of reference in the text is by the number of the reference only, enclosed in parentheses or brackets on the line.

Y. K. Belayev [8] gave the equivalent condition on the

f. Reference to a specific page

If reference is made to a specific page, the page number is given within the parentheses or brackets following the date or item number.

Chayes (1956, p. 351)

Leopold (51, p. 197)

[85, p. 112]

g. References by superscript numerals

Superscript numerals are used to indicate references in the text in any type of paper in the fields of chemistry and physics. Examples are given in the following section.

3. Footnotes

a. Reference footnotes

In journal articles in the fields of chemistry and physics, references to literature are usually given in footnotes. The writer of the article submits the footnotes on a separate sheet or sheets. When the article is published, the footnotes appear at the bottom of the pages of the article.

Superscript arabic numerals are used after the statements in the text and the same superscript numerals appear at the beginning of the footnotes. A superscript numeral is a numeral raised slightly above the line. Periods are not used after superscript numerals. In the text, the superscript numerals are placed after marks of punctuation.

```
...the interpolation schemes of Pines and Nozieres,27
```

```
The purpose has been discussed by Bienenstock and Brooks.38
```

Some journals prefer footnotes to be inserted between lines of the text. If this method is used, a footnote follows immediately the line of text containing the reference to it, and is separated from the text by a solid line above and below. Double spacing is used throughout.

```
detail by Borkman and Kearns.29  A noteworthy feature in all
```

```
    29R. Borkman and D. R. Kearns, J. Am. Chem. Soc., 88, 3467
(1966).
```

```
these systems is that singlet state quenching does not occur as

shown
```

b. Content footnotes

Content footnotes are often used in scientific papers. They are used to explain or amplify points in the text, or to add material of less importance than that in the text. They are numbered consecutively throughout the paper. They are indicated in the text by superscript arabic numerals as reference footnotes are. See page 111 for an example of a content footnote.

c. Numbering

If references to literature are given in footnotes, and content footnotes are also used, they are numbered consecutively in one sequence.

d. Indention

The first line of a footnote is indented five spaces from the left margin. Succeeding lines are flush with the left margin.

4. Abbreviations of journal titles

Titles of journals are abbreviated in citations in most scientific fields. Standard form for abbreviations should be followed.

Chemical Abstracts List of Periodicals gives abbreviations for journals in several scientific fields.

studied the photochemistry, and attempted to obtain a quantum
yield for the major product, assumed to be cyclopropyl propenyl
ketone. The results of the two studies yielded quantum yields
of 0.60 and 0.12, respectively, for the formation of the major
photoisomer.

The second principle objective of this study is to determine an accurate quantum yield for the major photoproduct in
the photolysis of dicyclopropyl ketone. The determination of
other products formed in primary steps would be undertaken.

GENERAL FEATURES OF VAPOR PHASE KETONE PHOTOCHEMISTRY

Spectroscopy of Carbonyl Chromophore

Photochemistry is the study of the chemical reactions of
molecules or atoms induced by absorption of electromagnetic
radiation. The most widely used region of the electromagnetic
spectrum corresponds to the visible and near ultraviolet
regions. The carbonyl chromophore,[1] among others, absorbs light
in the visible and ultraviolet regions and is of particular
interest to photochemists.

Aldehydes and ketones have been investigated more thor-
oughly than any other single class of compounds (2). This is
due in part to the availability of commercial light sources for
the visible and ultraviolet regions, and in part to theoretical
advances in the understanding of the carbonyl chromophore
(3,4,5).

---

[1]The term chromophore is a hold-over from early investiga-
tions of the absorption of light by organic dyes that were
highly colored; thus, the association of absorption with color,
even though the ketones under investigation are colorless!

Other sources of lists of abbreviations are:

American Chemical Society, *Handbook for Authors of Papers in the Journals of the American Chemical Society*
American Institute of Physics, *Style Manual for Preparation of Papers for Journals Published by the American Institute of Physics*
Chemical Society, London, *Handbook for Chemical Society Authors*
Conference of Biological Editors, *Style Manual for Biological Journals*
U.S. National Library of Medicine, *Cumulative Index Medicus*
U.S. Geological Survey, *Suggestions to Authors of the Reports of the United States Geological Survey*

5. *Documentation in specific fields*

There are variations in the form of documentation among the scientific fields as to indention, order of the author's name, location of the date of publication, inclusion of title, order of place of publication and publisher, inclusion of paging, punctuation, abbreviations, and capitalization.

Recommendations given in this section are in accordance with manuals and leading journals in the various scientific fields. Since journals within the same field may differ somewhat regarding the form of documentation, any one preparing an article for publication should observe the practice of the particular journal concerned. Many journals regularly include a section giving information for authors. For the purpose of the thesis, dissertation, or other reports prepared for schools, it is recommended that the student consult with his faculty adviser in the particular field or the thesis manuscript adviser to determine preferred form in his institution.

a. Biology, Botany, Zoology

References are given in a list at the end of an article, thesis, or dissertation in these fields. The left edge of the first line of a citation is flush with the left margin. The second and subsequent lines are indented five spaces from the left margin.

The author's name is inverted in a reference to a book or journal article. The name is followed by a period, year of publication, period, title of book or article, period.

In a reference to a book, the title is followed by the name of the publisher, comma, place of publication, period, and total paging indicated by the abbreviation *p.* following.

In a reference to a journal article, the title of the journal is abbreviated. The abbreviated title is followed by volume number, issue number (if necessary) in parentheses, colon, total paging of the article, period.

Only the first word, proper nouns, and proper adjectives are capitalized in book and article titles.

Book

```
Woodger, J. H. 1966.  Biological principles.  Humanities
     Press, New York.  496 p.
```

Journal article:

```
Newell, Irwin M. 1947.  Quantitative methods in
     biological and control studies of orchard mites.
     J. Econ. Entomol. 40(5): 683–689.
```

This form is according to the recommendations of:

Conference of Biological Editors, Committee on Form and Style. 1964. Style manual for biological journals. 2d ed. American Institute of Biological Sciences, Washington, D.C. 92 p.

In addition to documentation, the manual cited above also covers details of the mechanics of writing, such as grammar, spelling, punctuation, numerals, abbreviations and symbols; preparation of copy, including typing instructions, tables, illustrations, formulas, equations, nomenclature; and information on manuscripts submitted for publication, such as reviewing, copy editing, proofreading, and indexing.

b. Chemistry

Footnote form is used for references in the field of chemistry. References are listed at the end of a thesis or dissertation. In articles published in journals, the footnotes usually appear at the bottom of the pages. When an article is submitted for publication, the footnotes are placed on a separate sheet or sheets. Some journals place the references at the end of articles. Some prefer footnotes to be inserted between lines of text, as explained on page 110, when the manuscript is typed.

Superscript numerals are used in the text of an article, thesis, or dissertation to refer to the footnotes.

The first line of a footnote is indented five spaces from the left margin. The second and subsequent lines are flush with the left margin.

The author's name is in normal order, followed by a comma. The title of a book is enclosed in quotation marks and punctuated with a comma at the end. The first and last words and all nouns, pronouns, verbs, adjectives, and adverbs are capitalized in book titles. The edition, if any, is given after the title and is followed by a comma. The name of the publisher, place of publication, and year of publication, separated by commas, complete the citation. A period is used at the end.

In a reference to a journal article, the author's name is in normal order, followed by a comma. The title of the article is omitted. The title of the journal is abbreviated and underlined, and is followed by a comma. The volume number and page number (initial page only) are separated by a comma. The volume number is underlined. The year of publication, in parentheses, is given last, with a period after the second parenthesis.

Book:

    C. H. Hansch and G. K. Helmkamp, "Organic Chemistry,"
2d ed., McGraw—Hill, New York, 1963.

Journal article:

    R. C. Neuman, Jr. and V. Jonas, J. Am. Chem. Soc.,
90, 1970 (1968).

This form is according to the practice of leading chemical journals such as the *Journal of the American Chemical Society* and other journals published by the American Chemical Society.

Recommended for further information on problems of documentation is: American Chemical Society, "Handbook for Authors of Papers in the Journals of the American Chemical Society," American Chemical Society Publications, Washington, 1967. This handbook also includes other matters pertaining to the preparation of the manuscript such as spelling, punctuation, numbers, abbreviations, symbols, nomenclature, tables, and illustrations; the editorial process, including sections on manuscript review, processing of accepted manuscripts, reprints, and copying rights; a list of journals published by the American Chemical Society indicating types of material published by each; and several appendixes, including one containing hints to the typist.

Also recommended is: W. J. Gensler and K. D. Gensler, "Writing Guide for Chemists," McGraw-Hill, New York, 1961. This guide contains sections on style in technical writing, the laboratory notebook, the outline, writing the report, presenting experimental details, revision and proofreading, grammar, punctuation and italics, spelling and capitalization, nomenclature, abbreviations and symbols, forms for physical data, tables, figures, structural formulas, and documentation.

The mechanics of writing and matters of style are treated by: L. F. Fieser and M. Fieser, "Style Guide for Chemists," Reinhold, New York, 1960.

c. Geology

References are given at the end of an article, thesis, or dissertation. The first line of a citation is flush with the left margin. The second and subsequent lines are indented five spaces from the left edge of the first line.

In a reference to a book, the author's name inverted is followed by a comma, year of publication, comma, title of the book, colon, place of publication, comma, publisher, comma, total paging with the abbreviation *p.* following.

In a reference to a journal article, the order is: author's name inverted, comma, year of publication, comma, title of article, colon, title of the journal abbreviated, comma, volume number with the abbreviation *v.* before it, comma, total paging with the abbreviation *p.* preceding. A period is used at the end of the citation.

In titles of books and journal articles, only the first word, proper nouns, and proper adjectives are capitalized.

Book:

```
Clark, T. H., and Stearn, C. W., 1960, The geological
    evolution of North America: New York, Ronald
    Press, 434 p.
```

Journal article:

```
Murphy, M. A., 1960, Silurian reef complex and associated
    facies, central Nevada: J. Geol., v. 68, p. 117–139.
```

This form is according to the practice of the *Geological Society of America Bulletin* and the *Journal of Geology*.

The manual listed below is recommended for further information on problems of documentation, as well as details on form and content of reports, grammar and style in writing, topographic style, typing the manuscript, and correcting proof. While it is intended as a guide for the preparation of reports for the U.S. Geological Survey, much of the information is useful for writing theses, dissertations, and other research papers.

U.S. Geological Survey, 1958, Suggestions to authors of the reports of the United States
    Geological Survey: Washington, U.S. Govt. Printing Office, 255 p.

d. Mathematics

A modified footnote form is used for references in the field of mathematics. The references are given in a list at the end of the paper, whether it is a thesis, dissertation, journal article, or other type of research paper. The first line of a citation is indented five spaces from the left margin. The second and subsequent lines are flush with the left margin.

The author's name is in normal order and is followed by a comma. The title, either of a book or a journal article, is underlined and followed by a comma. In a reference to a book, the publisher's name is given after the title, then place of publication, and year. These items are separated by commas. A period closes the citation.

In a reference to a journal article, the title of the journal is abbreviated. It is followed, without punctuation, by the volume number underlined, the year of publication in parentheses, comma, total paging, and a period.

Only the first word, proper nouns, and proper adjectives are capitalized in titles of books and articles.

Book:

> H. G. Tucker, <u>An introduction to probability and mathematical statistics</u>, Academic Press, New York, 1962.

Journal article:

> C. J. A. Halberg, <u>Semigroups of matrices defining linked operators with different spectra</u>, Pacific J. Math. <u>13</u> (1963), 1187–1191.

This form is according to the practice of the Transactions of the American Mathematical Society. It is recommended to writers of theses and dissertations.

e. Physics

Footnote form is used for references in the field of physics. References are listed at the end of a thesis or dissertation. In journal articles the footnotes usually appear at the bottom of the pages. The writer of a journal article, however, submits the footnotes on a separate sheet or sheets. Some journals place the references at the end of articles.

Superscript numerals are used in the text of an article, thesis, or dissertation to refer to the footnotes.

The first line of a citation is indented five spaces from the left margin. The second and subsequent lines are flush with the left margin.

The author's name is in normal order and is followed by a comma. The title of a book is underlined. The first and last words and all nouns, pronouns, verbs, adjectives and adverbs are capitalized. The name of the publisher, place of publication, and year are placed in parentheses. Commas separate these items and a comma is used after the second parenthesis. The abbreviation *p.* is given before the page number in a reference to a book. A period closes the citation.

In a reference to a journal article, the title of the article is omitted. The title of the journal is abbreviated. It is followed immediately by the volume number underlined. A comma separates the volume number from the page number (initial page only). The year of publication is placed in parentheses. A period is used after the second parenthesis.

Book:

W. H. Barkas, <u>Nuclear Research Emulsions</u> (Academic
Press, New York, 1963), p. 88.

Journal article:

R. R. Hewitt and T. T. Taylor, Phys. Rev. <u>125</u>, 524(1962).

This form is according to the practice of the *Physical Review*, the *American Journal of Physics*, *Reviews of Modern Physics*, and other journals in this field.

American Institute of Physics, *Style Manual for Guidance in the Preparation of Papers for Journals Published by the American Institute of Physics* (American Institute of Physics, New York, 1959) gives information on the preparation of a scientific paper, including writing of the paper and the abstract, presenting the manuscript, and proofreading the paper; general style, including grammar, punctuation, spelling, abbreviations, and capitalization; presentation of mathematical expressions; special characters and signs; and preparation of illustrations. Documentation is treated briefly.

f. Psychology

In the field of psychology, references are given in a list at the end of an article, thesis, dissertation, or other research paper. The first line of a citation is flush with the left margin. The second and subsequent lines are indented five spaces from the left edge of the first line.

Authors' names are in inverted order, with only the initial or initials rather than full spelling of first names. In a reference to a book, the title is underlined and followed by a period. The place of publication is followed by a colon, name of publisher, comma, year of publication, period.

In a reference to a journal article, the author's name is followed by the title of the article, period, title of the journal spelled out in full and underlined, comma, year of publication, comma, volume number underlined, comma, complete paging, period.

Only the first word, proper nouns, and proper adjectives in titles of books and articles are capitalized.

Book:

Andreas, B. G. <u>Experimental psychology</u>. New York:
    Wiley, 1960.

Journal article:

Nachman, M. The inheritance of saccharin preference.
    <u>Journal of Comparative and Physiological Psychology</u>,
    1959, <u>52</u>, 451–457.

This form is according to the recommendations of the manual listed below. It is recommended to students for the preparation of papers, theses, and dissertations as well as to authors of articles to be published in journals. It includes sections on organization and writing, quality and style of writing, title and headings, general style, tabular presentation, auxiliary publication, preparation of figures, references, typing the manuscript, and correction of proofs.

American Psychological Association. *Publication Manual of the American Psychological Association.* (Rev. ed.) Washington, D.C.: APA, 1967.

VI
Typing
the Manuscript

If the writer does not type his own paper, he should be sure that the typist follows instructions to meet the requirements of the particular institution or publication concerned. It is the responsibility of the writer to check the manuscript carefully to be sure it is in correct form before turning it over to the typist.

Detailed instructions for form are given throughout the manual for the writer to follow as he prepares the manuscript. The instructions concerning form in this section are presented in summary or outline form principally for quick reference for the typist.

A. TYPEWRITER

A standard typewriter with plain type face should be used. A standard electric typewriter produces the best results. Pica size type is usually preferred, but elite type is accepted by some institutions. For large tables and charts elite type may be preferable. The keyboard should include foreign accents and square brackets in addition to the keys normally found on a typewriter.

B. TYPEWRITER RIBBON

A good quality, all black typewriter ribbon should be used and changed often enough to assure even density of type. Nylon or carbon ribbons produce clearer type than cotton or silk ribbons.

C. PAPER

A good quality of white opaque paper, size $8\frac{1}{2}$ x 11 inches, should be used. Bond paper of 16- or 20-pound weight is recommended. Some institutions require special thesis paper with colored margin lines for theses and dissertations. Only one side of the sheets should be used.

D. CARBON PAPER

If carbon copies are made, a good quality of black nonsmudge carbon paper should be used and changed frequently. Sufficient carbon paper for typing the entire paper should be acquired before typing is started so that weight and color will be uniform. It is advisable to make one carbon copy even though another type of duplication is to be used, because of the possibility of loss or damage to the original typed copy.

E. CORRECTIONS

Neatness in typing is essential. Corrections should be kept to a minimum and should be made so neatly that they are not noticeable. Corrections may be made with a good typing eraser. They should not be made with ink or by typing one letter over another. The addition of letters or words in the space between lines is not acceptable. The use of correction tape or white correction fluid is acceptable for corrections on copy to be duplicated. Any extensive corrections should be made by retyping.

F. MARGINS

Recommended margins are $1\frac{1}{2}$ inches at the left side of each page, 1 inch at the right side, and $1\frac{1}{4}$ inches at top and bottom. The same margins should be observed on all pages including those containing tables, charts, and illustrations.

The wider margin of $1\frac{1}{2}$ inches at the left side is necessary for binding theses and dissertations. It is also desirable for undergraduate papers that are to be placed in binders. Care should be taken to observe the $1\frac{1}{2}$ inch margin at the right edge of facing pages containing legends for illustrations. The right edge is the binding edge for facing pages.

G. FOOTNOTES

Pages containing footnotes should be planned so that the correct amount of space is allowed. Footnotes should not run into the bottom margin or continue on another page. A guide sheet with numbers indicating the number of lines on the page is helpful. Guide sheets may be purchased, or they can be made by measuring off the top and bottom margins on a sheet of paper and numbering the remaining lines with the typewriter along the right hand edge of the paper. Numbering should start with one at the bottom line. This sheet can be placed under the bottom sheet of typing paper and rolled into the typewriter with the right edge extending to show the line numbers. If preferred, the guide sheet can be made on onion skin and placed between the top sheet of typing paper and the carbon paper so the numbers can be read through the top sheet. The number of lines necessary for the footnotes, the number of spaces between the text and the first footnote, and between footnotes (see page 50) should be added together. This will indicate the last line on which text should be typed on that page.

Further instructions for typing footnotes are given on pages 51–74.

H. INDENTION

The first line of a paragraph should be indented five spaces from the left margin. If material is to be indented further within the text, each indention is five additional spaces. See page 3 for an illustration.

See the following pages for instructions for the indention of material other than the text itself.

Footnotes, page 50
Bibliography, page 75
Quotations, pages 4–5
Table captions, page 93
Figure legends, page 99

I. SPACING

In general a research paper is double-spaced. The items listed in the first group below are single-spaced in any type of paper prepared for schools. In material submitted for publication these items are also double-spaced. Items in the third group below are triple-spaced without exception.

1. Single-spacing is used in:

a. References in footnotes and bibliography
b. Captions for tables
c. Legends for illustrations
d. Centered and side headings of more than one line
e. Quotations set off from the text
f. Tables (Material in tables may be single- or double-spaced.)
g. Appendixes

2. Double-spacing is used:

a. In the text
b. Between titles in the table of contents, list of tables, and list of illustrations
c. Between items in footnotes and the bibliography
d. Between side headings and the first line of text following
e. Between two subheadings with no lines of text between
f. In tables (Material in tables may be single- or double-spaced.)
g. Between a table caption and the top line of the table
h. Between the bottom line of a table and the first footnote
i. Between the bottom of an illustration and the figure number (or figure number and legend depending upon the style used)
j. Between a figure legend and the first footnote
k. In material prepared for publication, including the items listed above which are single-spaced in research papers prepared for schools

3. Triple-spacing is used:

a. Between a chapter number and a chapter title
b. Between a chapter title and the first line of text below it
c. Between headings for other major divisions such as the preface, introduction, bibliography, and appendix and the first line below
d. Between the headings for the table of contents, list of tables, and list of illustrations and the first entry below these headings
e. Above and below a centered heading within a chapter
f. Between a side heading and the preceding line of text

4. Spacing after punctuation

a. Leave one space following
   commas
   semicolons
   periods after initials in names of persons

b. Leave two spaces following
   colons
   exclamation marks
   question marks
   periods at the end of sentences
c. Leave no space before or after hyphens and dashes

J. PAGE NUMBERING

Preliminary pages are numbered with lowercase roman numerals centered at the bottom of the page ¾ inch above the edge. The title page is counted in the pagination but the numeral is not actually typed on the page. Actual numbering begins with *ii*. If there is a copyright notice, it is neither numbered nor counted.

The main body of the text is numbered with arabic numerals beginning with the introduction and continuing throughout, including text, illustrations, bibliography, and appendixes. In the case of full-page illustrations with legends on facing pages, both pages are numbered. Numerals are centered at the top of the page ¾ inch below the edge, except that the first page of the text and every page with a major heading, such as the first page of chapters, bibliography, and appendix, are numbered at the bottom of the page with numbers centered ¾ inch above the edge. All page numbers should appear without periods, parentheses, or dashes.

K. UNDERLINING

1. Titles

Titles of books, journals, and newspapers are underlined in footnotes, bibliography, and in the text. Titles of pamphlets, bulletins, and documents are also underlined.

2. Headings

Centered and side headings within chapters may be underlined for emphasis.

3. Foreign words, phrases, and abbreviations

Foreign words and phrases used in an English text are underlined except words in a quotation entirely in a foreign language or words which have become anglicized through frequent use. Abbreviations of foreign words and phrases are also underlined. Examples are: *et al.*, *ibid.*, *op. cit.*, and *loc. cit.* Foreign titles and foreign names of institutions, persons, and places are not underlined.

L. PROOFREADING

The entire paper should be carefully proofread. Each page should be proofread before it is taken out of the typewriter. This is important for making corrections and for checking for any omissions of material before proceeding to the next page. If the paper is typed by someone other than the writer, the writer should also proofread every page.

Appendix
Research
Methods and Sources

A. SELECTING A SUBJECT

The subject for a research paper may be assigned by the instructor, or the student may be free to choose a subject of interest to him. In the latter case, the undergraduate student, especially, should be careful to choose a subject not too broad in scope, not too technical for him to handle well, one for which sufficient material can be found, and one for which material is available in several types of publications.

B. SOURCES OF INFORMATION

The search for information should involve several reference sources. The student should become familiar with those sources and their location in the library he is using. Reference librarians may be consulted for information on the sources available and for assistance in their use.

The card catalog, bibliographies, indexes, and abstract journals are explained in this section as tools for finding references on particular subjects. Before beginning the search for references, it may be desirable, especially for the undergraduate student, to do some preliminary reading for an overview of the subject selected. Encyclopedias, both general and in special subject fields, and histories in the subject fields are useful for this purpose.

1. Card catalog

After the student has done some preliminary reading for an overview of his subject, the next step is to find what books are available. The card catalog of a library lists books under authors' names, under titles, and under subjects. The approach for finding material for a paper will usually be by subject. Students may need assistance from a reference librarian in using the card catalog, especially in determining the best subject headings for individual topics.

The sample catalog cards, shown in Figures A–1, A–2, and A–3, illustrate the different types of cards for a book and the information they give.

Cataloging form differs from standard bibliographic form in spacing, capitalization, and punctuation. The forms for footnotes and bibliography, as explained and illustrated in the section on documentation, pages 48–88, should be used in a research paper.

PR461
H52
Hicks, Granville, 1901–
     Figures of transition; a study of British literature at the
end of the nineteenth century, by Granville Hicks.   New
York, The Macmillan company, 1939.

     xv p., 1 l., 326 p.   22 cm.

     "First printing."
     Bibliography : p. 317–322.

     1. English literature—19th cent.—Hist. & crit.   i. Title.

     PR461.H5   820.903   40—669

     Library of Congress   [55x1]

FIGURE A–1. Author card.

PR461
H52
          Figures of transition

Hicks, Granville, 1901–
     Figures of transition; a study of British literature at the
end of the nineteenth century, by Granville Hicks.   New
York, The Macmillan company, 1939.

     xv p., 1 l., 326 p.   22 cm.

     "First printing."
     Bibliography : p. 317–322.

     1. English literature—19th cent.—Hist. & crit.   i. Title.

     PR461.H5   820.903   40—669

     Library of Congress   [55x1]

FIGURE A–2. Title card.

PR461
H52
          English literature–19th century–History and
              criticism
Hicks, Granville, 1901–
     Figures of transition; a study of British literature at the
end of the nineteenth century, by Granville Hicks.   New
York, The Macmillan company, 1939.

     xv p., 1 l., 326 p.   22 cm.

     "First printing."
     Bibliography : p. 317–322.

     1. English literature—19th cent.—Hist. & crit.   i. Title.

     PR461.H5   820.903   40—669

     Library of Congress   [55x1]

FIGURE A–3. Subject card.

2. *Bibliographies*

If the student wishes to find books in addition to those listed in the card catalog of the library he is using, he may consult bibliographies—both general and in special subject areas.

a. General bibliographies

U.S. Library of Congress. *Library of Congress Catalog . . . Books: Subjects.* Ann Arbor, Mich.: J. W. Edwards, 1950– .

> Issued quarterly with annual and five-year cumulations. A subject bibliography of works received and cataloged by the Library of Congress and other American libraries participating in its cooperative cataloging program. Complements the Library of Congress author catalog, 1942–1953, and *National Union Catalog*, 1958– .

Cumulative Book Index. New York: H. W. Wilson Company, 1933– .

> Published monthly with cumulations. A comprehensive list of books in English with entries under authors, titles, and subjects. Gives bibliographic information, including price. Preceded by *United States Catalog*, 4th ed., 1928, covering books in print in 1928.

b. Subject bibliographies

Subject bibliographies are lists of books and other types of publications on particular subjects. Bibliographies are available on many subjects from small specialized areas to broad fields of knowledge. They are listed in the card catalog of a library under the subject heading followed by a dash and the word *Bibliography*. Examples are: Air pollution-Bibliography; Education, Higher-Bibliography; United States-History-Bibliography.

For subject bibliographies in addition to those listed in the card catalog, the bibliographies of bibliographies listed below may be used.

Besterman, Theodore. *A World Bibliography of Bibliographies and of Bibliographical Catalogues, Calendars, Abstracts, Digests, Indexes and the Like.* 4th ed., rev. and enl. 5 vols. Lausanne: Societas Bibliographica, 1965–1966.

> A classified list of 117,000 separately published bibliographies. International in scope. Volume 5 is an index of authors, editors, translators, serial and anonymous works, libraries, archives, and patents.

Bibliographic Index: A Cumulative Bibliography of Bibliographies. New York: H. W. Wilson Company, 1945– .

> Issued semiannually with cumulations. An alphabetical subject list of separately published bibliographies and bibliographies in books and periodicals.

Listed below are bibliographies of broad coverage, representative of the major subject fields.

Humanities

Lucas, Edna L. *Harvard List of Books on Art.* Cambridge, Mass.: Harvard University Press, 1952.

> Major sections are Reference Handbooks and Indexes, Iconography and Symbolism, History and Esthetics, Architecture, Sculpture, Painting, Graphic Arts and Illumination, Minor Arts, and Individual Artists.

New York Metropolitan Museum of Art. Library. *Library Catalog.* 25 vols. Boston: G. K. Hall & Co., 1960. Supplements, 1962– .
> A photographic reproduction in book form of the card catalog of this library's collection of 145,000 volumes on art and related fields. Subject, author, and title entries.

Modern Language Association of America. *M.L.A. International Bibliography.* New York: Kraus Reprint Corp., 1964– .
> Issued annually. Entitled *American Bibliography*, 1921–1955, and limited to American writers in the field of modern languages and literatures. Beginning in 1956 the coverage became international including writers in English, French, German, Spanish, Italian, Portuguese, Scandinavian, and Dutch. Also issued as annual supplements to *PMLA*, vol. 39– .

Blanck, Jacob N. *Bibliography of American Literature.* New York: Yale University Press, 1955– . (In progress)
> A selective bibliography of American authors which will include approximately 300 writers from the American Revolution to 1930. Material for each includes first editions of books, reprints containing changes, list of biographical, bibliographical, and critical works.

Bateson, F. W., ed. *Cambridge Bibliography of English Literature.* 5 vols. New York: Macmillan Company, 1941–1957.
> A comprehensive bibliography arranged chronologically and under periods by literary form and large class groups. References under each author include bibliographies, collected editions, separate works, and biographical and critical works.

Baker, Blanch M. *Theatre and Allied Arts: A Guide to Books Dealing with the History, Criticism, and Technic of the Drama and Theatre and Related Arts and Crafts.* New York: H. W. Wilson Company, 1952.
> An annotated list of 6,000 titles in a classified arrangement with author and subject indexes.

New York Public Library. Research Libraries. *Catalog of the Theatre and Drama Collection.* Boston: G. K. Hall & Co., 1967.
> Part I, Drama Collection: Author Listing (6 vols.), Listing by Cultural Origin (6 vols.), lists 120,000 plays in western languages. Part II, Theatre Collection: Books on the Theatre (9 vols.), lists 23,500 volumes and includes citations for selected periodical articles. Author, title, and subject entries.

The American Historical Association's Guide to Historical Literature. New York: Macmillan Company, 1961.
> A selective, annotated bibliography of fundamental treatises and source material, arranged by large subjects and geographical areas. Included in each section are bibliographies; encyclopedias and works of reference; geographies and atlases; anthropologic, demographic, and linguistic works; printed collections of sources; histories; biographies; government publications; university, academy, and society publications; and periodicals. The 1931 edition includes references to reviews.

International Bibliography of Historical Sciences. Paris: International Committee of Historical Sciences, 1930–   .

> Issued annually. A classified list including political, constitutional, religious, cultural, economic, and social history, and international relations.

Darrell, Robert D. *Schirmer's Guide to Books on Music and Musicians: A Practical Bibliography.* New York: G. Schirmer, 1951.

> An annotated guide to books in English on all aspects of music. Appendixes list books in French, German, Italian, Spanish, and Latin. Subject and author entries arranged alphabetically, with complete information under subject.

New York Public Library. Reference Department. *Dictionary Catalog of the Music Collection.* 33 vols. Boston: G. K. Hall & Co., 1964. Supplements, 1966–   .

> Catalog of a large collection of literature on the entire field of music and scores covering a broad range of musical style and history. Author, title, and subject entries.

Los Angeles. University of Southern California. Hoose Library of Philosophy. *Catalog.* 6 vols. Boston: G. K. Hall & Co., 1968.

> An author, title, and subject catalog of 37,000 volumes ranging from medieval manuscripts to the works of present-day philosophers.

Répertoire bibliographique de la philosophie. Louvain: Éditions de l'Institut Supérieur de Philosophie, 1949–   .

> Issued quarterly. A comprehensive list of books and articles on philosophy published in several countries. In a classified arrangement with annual author indexes.

Diehl, Katharine S. *Religions, Mythologies, Folklores: An Annotated Bibliography.* 2d ed. New York: Scarecrow Press, 1962.

> Includes reference books, bibliographies, histories, anthologies, biographies, and journals. In a classified arrangement with author and title index.

Union Theological Seminary Library, New York City. *Shelf List.* 10 vols. Boston, Mass.: G. K. Hall & Co., 1960.

> A classified list of 350,000 volumes especially strong in historical material.

———. *Alphabetical Arrangement of Main Entries from the Shelf List.* 10 vols. Boston: G. K. Hall & Co., 1960.

> Serves as an author catalog for the *Shelf List.*

Social sciences

American Behavioral Scientist. *ABS Guide to Recent Publications in the Social and Behavioral Sciences.* New York: American Behavioral Scientist, 1965.

> A selective, annotated bibliography of 6,700 books and articles, interdisciplinary in coverage. Arranged alphabetically by author, with a topical and methodological index, a book title index, and a proper name index. Kept up-to-date by *New Studies: A Guide to Recent Publications in the Social and Behavioral Sciences,* published monthly, and by the annual *ABS Guide Supplement.*

London Bibliography of the Social Sciences. London: London School of Economics,
  1931–   . (In progress).
    The most extensive subject bibliography in this field. Entries are arranged alpha-
    betically by subject, giving author, title, paging, date, and location.

U.S. Department of Health, Education, and Welfare. Library. *Author-Title Catalog of the
  Department Library.* 29 vols. Boston: G. K. Hall & Co., 1966.

————. *Subject Catalog of the Department.* 20 vols. Boston: G. K. Hall & Co., 1965.
    A photoreproduction of the card catalog of the library's collection of 500,000
    volumes, especially strong in education, the social sciences, and a research collec-
    tion in law, and the most complete set of departmental and operating agencies'
    publications.

Harvard University. Peabody Museum of Archaeology and Ethnology. Library. *Catalogue.* 54 vols. Boston: G. K. Hall & Co., 1963.
    A photographic reproduction in book form of the library card catalog for 82,000
    volumes and pamphlets. The author section (vols. 1–26) includes journal articles,
    compilations, and proceedings of congresses, as well as books. The subject sec-
    tion (vols. 1–28) covers general and physical anthropology, ethnology, and pre-
    historic archaeology.

International Bibliography of Social and Cultural Anthropology. Chicago: Aldine Publishing
  Company, 1955–   .
    A classified bibliography published annually. Includes books, articles, reports,
    and government publications in several languages from many countries. Author
    and subject indexes.

Cumulative Bibliography of Economic Books. New York: Gordon and Breach Science
  Publishers, 1965–   .
    Volume I is a cumulation of the lists in *Economics Library Selections*, Ser. I and
    II, published by the Department of Political Economy, Johns Hopkins Uni-
    versity, 1954–1962. A classified list of more than 7,600 items. Author index. The
    Department of Economics, University of Pittsburgh, has published the current
    series since 1963 and edited this volume.

International Bibliography of Economics. Chicago: Aldine Publishing Company, 1955–   .
    An annual bibliography of books, periodical articles, pamphlets, and govern-
    ment publications in several languages. In a classified arrangement with author
    and subject indexes.

Harmon, Robert B. *Political Science: A Bibliographical Guide to the Literature.* New York:
  Scarecrow Press, 1965. Supplement, 1968.
    Major sections on general research materials; political science and the study of
    politics; comparative government; state and local government; political parties,
    public opinion, and electoral processes; political theory; law and jurisprudence;
    public administration; and international relations. Appendixes list periodicals,
    government documents, and agencies and institutions engaged in political
    research.

International Bibliography of Political Science. Chicago: Aldine Publishing Company, 1954– .
> An annual bibliography including books, periodical articles, government publications, and reports from various countries in several languages. In a classified arrangement with author and subject indexes.

International Bibliography of Sociology. Chicago: Aldine Publishing Company, 1952– .
> An annual listing of books, periodical articles, pamphlets, and government publications in several languages. In a classified arrangement with author and subject indexes.

Current Sociology. Oxford: Basil Blackwell, 1957– .
> An international bibliography of sociology published quarterly. Each issue contains a trend report and a bibliography on a particular aspect of sociology.

American Geographical Society of New York. *Research Catalog.* 15 vols. Boston: G. K. Hall & Co., 1962. Map Supplement, 1962.
> A photographic reproduction in book form of the card catalog of books, periodical articles, pamphlets, and government publications, totaling 219,000 entries. Kept up-to-date by *Current Geographical Publications.*

American Geographical Society of New York. *Current Geographical Publications.* New York: American Geographical Society, 1938– .
> A classified listing of books, pamphlets, periodical articles, government publications, and maps. Published monthly with annual subject, author, and regional indexes.

Columbia University. Law Library. *Dictionary Catalog.* 28 vols. Boston: G. K. Hall & Co., 1968.
> Catalog of a collection of 465,000 volumes, especially strong in legal literature of the United States and the British Commonwealth, with excellent coverage of Roman and medieval law, the legal literature of France, Germany, Austria, Italy, and Spain, and African law. To be supplemented.

Current Legal Bibliography. Cambridge, Mass.: Harvard Law School Library, 1961– .
> Lists books, articles, and monographs received by the Harvard Law School Library. Issued nine times per year. Cumulated by the *Annual Legal Bibliography* (Cambridge, Mass.: Harvard Law School Library, 1967–).

Science—general

McGraw-Hill Basic Bibliography of Science and Technology. New York: McGraw-Hill Book Company, 1966.
> A classified listing of books under more than 7,000 specific headings corresponding to those of the articles in the *McGraw-Hill Encyclopedia of Science and Technology.* Cross references to other headings are included. Items are briefly annotated. Emphasis is on recently published books.

Biological sciences

U.S. Department of Agriculture. Library. *Plant Science Catalog: Botany Subject Index*. 15 vols. Boston: MICROphotography Co., 1958.
> International in scope. Includes references to botanical literature in books and serials from the earliest times. Also includes references to related subjects of interest to botanists.

Harvard University. Museum of Comparative Zoology. Library. *Catalogue*. 8 vols. Boston: G. K. Hall & Co., 1968.
> Reproduction of a main entry catalog of 250,000 volumes, manuscripts, photographs, and maps in the fields of zoology, paleozoology, and geology relating to paleozoology.

Zoological Record. London: Zoological Society of London, 1865– .
> A comprehensive listing of the zoological literature of the world. Issued annually in twenty sections, each of which records the literature relating to a class or phylum of the animal kingdom. The listing in each section is by author with a subject index.

U.S. National Library of Medicine. *Current Catalog*. Washington, D.C.: Government Printing Office, 1966– .
> Issued biweekly with quarterly and annual cumulations. In two sections, a subject section and a name section. Includes citations to monographs, new serial titles, and audiovisual materials published in the last two years.

Harvard University. *Harvard List of Books in Psychology*. 3d ed. Cambridge: Harvard University Press, 1964.
> A classified, annotated list of 704 books arranged in 31 sections.

U.S. National Agricultural Library. *Dictionary Catalog of the National Agricultural Library, 1862–1965*. New York: Rowman and Littlefield, 1967– . (In progress)
> Author, title, and subject entries for monographs, serials, and analytics. Descriptive information is reproduced as it appears in the card catalog. Supplemented by the *National Agricultural Library Catalog* (New York: Rowman and Littlefield, 1966–), a monthly list of all additions to the collection.

U.S. National Agricultural Library. *Bibliography of Agriculture*. Washington, D.C.: Government Printing Office, 1942– .
> Lists the literature of agriculture and allied sciences received in the National Agricultural Library. Limited to currently published material in agricultural fields of major interest to the U.S. Department of Agriculture. In a classified arrangement with subject and author indexes. Issued monthly. Annual cumulative indexes.

Physical sciences

Bolton, Henry C. *Select Bibliography of Chemistry, 1492–1902*. 4 vols. Washington, D.C.: Smithsonian Institution, 1893–1904.
> Basic list plus supplements cover 1492–1902. In eight sections: (1) Bibliography; (2) Dictionaries; (3) History; (4) Biography; (5) Chemistry, Pure and Applied; (6) Alchemy; (7) Periodicals; (8) Academic Dissertations.

U.S. Geological Survey. Library. *Catalog of the United States Geological Survey Library.* 25 vols. Boston: G. K. Hall & Co., 1964.

> An author, title, and subject catalog of the largest geological library in the world, with comprehensive holdings in geology, paleontology, petrology, mineralogy, ground and surface water, cartography, and mineral resources, and selective holdings in related fields.

U.S. Geological Survey. *Bibliography of North American Geology.* Washington, D.C.: Government Printing Office, 1896– .

> Issued in the *Bulletin* series. Covers 1732 to date. Includes geology, paleontology, petrology, and mineralogy. Arranged by author with subject and area index.

Geological Society of America. *Bibliography and Index of Geology Exclusive of North America.* Washington, D.C.: Geological Society of America, 1934– .

> An annual compilation of references to books, monographs, papers, and articles dealing with the geology of all parts of the world except North America.

Parke, Nathan G. *Guide to the Literature of Mathematics and Physics Including Related Works on Engineering Science.* 2d rev. ed. New York: Dover Publications, 1958.

> A bibliography of more than 5,000 entries listed under 120 subject headings arranged alphabetically. Also includes a section on literature-searching. Author and subject indexes.

Goldman, Sylvia. *Guide to the Literature of Engineering, Mathematics, and the Physical Sciences.* 2d ed. Silver Spring, Md.: Johns Hopkins University, Applied Physics Laboratory, 1964.

> The main section is a listing of general books under subject headings arranged alphabetically. Includes shorter sections on abstracting journals, indexes, periodicals, and reference books.

Whitford, Robert H. *Physics Literature: A Reference Manual.* 2d ed. Metuchen, N.J.: Scarecrow Press, 1968.

> A survey of physics literature at the college level. Describes the types and forms available, selects a representative working collection, and outlines library methods.

New York. Engineering Societies Library. *Classed Subject Catalog.* 13 vols. Boston: G. K. Hall & Co., 1963. Supplements, 1964– .

> A catalog of the books, pamphlets, bulletins, and reports of the largest engineering library in the United States. Alphabetical index to the catalog in a separate volume.

3. Periodical indexes

Periodical indexes are guides to information in periodical articles. They provide the key to important research literature both current and historical. Articles are listed in these indexes by subjects. Some indexes list articles by subjects and authors. Some list books, pamphlets, and government publications in addition to periodical articles.

Below is a sample entry from the *Social Sciences and Humanities Index*, with explanation.

```
LITERATURE, Renaissance
   German renaissance literature. H. Jantz. Mod Lang Notes.
   81:398–436 O'66
```

LITERATURE, Renaissance—subject heading
German renaissance literature—title of article
H. Jantz—author of article
Mod Lang Notes—*Modern Language Notes*—title of periodical
81—volume number of periodical
398–436—paging of article
0 '66—October, 1966—date of publication

References to articles as given in periodical indexes are not in standard bibliographic form. The forms for footnotes and bibliography, as explained and illustrated in the section on documentation, pages 48–88, should be used in a research paper.

a. General periodical indexes

Readers' Guide to Periodical Literature. New York: H. W. Wilson Company, 1915–   .
    Issued biweekly with cumulations. Subject, author, and some title coverage, especially of the popular type periodicals.

Nineteenth Century Readers' Guide to Periodical Literature. 2 vols. New York: H. W. Wilson Company, 1944.
    A subject and author index to fifty-one periodicals, mainly general and literary. Covers the period 1890–1899, with supplementary indexing 1900–1922.

Poole's Index to Periodical Literature. 6 vols. New York: Houghton Mifflin, 1882. Reprint ed. New York: Peter Smith, 1938.
    A subject index to periodicals of the nineteenth century (1802–1906). Includes references to book reviews.

Annual Magazine Subject Index. 42 vols. Boston: F. W. Faxon Company, 1909–1950.
    Reprinted as *Cumulative Magazine Subject Index, 1907–1949,* 2 vols. (Boston: G. K. Hall & Co., 1964). A subject index to a selected list of American, Canadian, and English periodicals and society publications. Covers periodicals not included in other indexes.

b. Periodical indexes in special subject areas

Humanities

Social Sciences and Humanities Index. New York: H. W. Wilson Company, 1965–   .
    Issued quarterly with cumulations. A subject and author index to more than 200 scholarly journals in these fields. Continues *International Index* (New York: H. W. Wilson Company, 1916–1965).

British Humanities Index. London: Library Association, 1963–   .
    Issued quarterly with cumulations. A subject index to British periodicals. Separate author index section. Continues *Subject Index to Periodicals* (London: Library Association, 1919–1961).

Art Index. New York: H. W. Wilson Company, 1929–   .
    Issued quarterly with cumulations. An author and subject index to a selected list of periodicals in archaeology, architecture, art history, arts and crafts, fine arts, graphic arts, industrial design, interior decoration, photography and films, planning and landscape design, and related subjects.

Music Index. Detroit, Mich.: Information Service, Inc., 1949– .

    Issued monthly with annual cumulations and a separate annual subject heading list. A subject-author index to current music periodical literature. Includes references to reviews of books, published music, performances, and records.

Guide to the Performing Arts. New York: Scarecrow Press, 1960– .

    An annual index of articles and illustrations from journals dealing with music, opera, the dance, the theatre, and television.

Philosopher's Index. Bowling Green, Ohio: Bowling Green University, 1967– .

    Issued monthly with cumulations. A subject and author index to all major American and British philosophical periodicals, selected journals in other languages, and related interdisciplinary publications.

Index to Religious Periodical Literature. Chicago: American Theological Library Association, 1953– .

    Issued annually with cumulations. An author and subject index to 127 periodicals in this field. Includes an author index of book reviews.

Social sciences

Social Sciences and Humanities Index. New York: H. W. Wilson Company, 1965– .

    Issued quarterly with cumulations. A subject and author index to more than 200 scholarly journals in these fields. Continues *International Index* (New York: H. W. Wilson Company, 1916–1965).

Public Affairs Information Service Bulletin. New York: Public Affairs Information Service, 1915– .

    Issued weekly with cumulations. A subject index to books, government publications, pamphlets, and periodical articles in political science, government, legislation, economics, sociology, and other social sciences fields.

Anthropological Index to Current Periodicals in the Library of the Royal Anthropological Institute. London: Royal Anthropological Institute, 1963– .

    A quarterly index to periodicals from various countries of the world. References are arranged in sections by continent and each section is subdivided by general, physical anthropology, archaeology, cultural anthropology, ethnography, and linguistics.

Business Periodicals Index. New York: H. W. Wilson Company, 1958– .

    Issued monthly with cumulations. A subject index to the fields of accounting, advertising, banking and finance, general business, insurance, labor and management, marketing and purchasing, office management, public administration, taxation, specific businesses, industries, and trades. Preceded by *Industrial Arts Index* (New York: H. W. Wilson Company, 1913–1957).

Index of Economic Journals. Homewood, Ill.: Richard D. Irwin, Inc., 1961– .

    An author and subject index of English language articles in major professional economic journals published since 1886. Beginning with volume VII, published 1967, each volume covers a two-year period. Earlier volumes cover longer periods.

Education Index. New York: H. W. Wilson Company, 1932– .
> A cumulative index to a selected list of educational periodicals, books, pamphlets, and government publications, covering the entire field of education. Volumes for July, 1961–June, 1969 are subject indexes only. Other volumes include author and subject entries and references to book reviews. Issued monthly with cumulations.

Index to Legal Periodicals. New York: H. W. Wilson Company in cooperation with the American Association of Law Libraries, 1909– .
> Issued monthly with cumulations. In three parts: Subject and Author Index, Table of Cases, and Book Review Index.

Science—general

Applied Science and Technology Index. New York: H. W. Wilson Company, 1958– .
> Issued monthly with cumulations. A subject index to periodicals in the fields of aeronautics, automation, chemistry, construction, electricity, engineering, geology, metallurgy, industrial and mechanical arts, machinery, physics, transportation, and related subjects. Preceded by *Industrial Arts Index* (New York: H. W. Wilson Company, 1913–1957).

Science Citation Index. Philadelphia: Institute for Scientific Information, 1961– .
> A science literature index, including citations to journals, books, meetings, dissertations, reports, contracts, patents, circulars, and personal communications from several countries, covering every major subject category in science. Arranged alphabetically by author, grouping under each reference all authors and papers referring to that work since its publication. Each of the author's cited works, accompanied by its citing authors, is arranged chronologically. Issued quarterly, with annual cumulations in three parts: Citation Index, Source Index, and Permuterm Subject Index.

Biological sciences

Biological and Agricultural Index. New York: H. W. Wilson Company, 1964– .
> Issued monthly with cumulations. A subject index to periodicals in the fields of biology, agriculture, and related sciences. Continues *Agricultural Index* (New York: H. W. Wilson Company, 1919–1964).

Behavior and Physiology Index. Kansas City, Mo.: Science Search Associates, 1967– .
> A monthly index to the literature of physiological psychology. Annual cumulative author and subject indexes.

Index Medicus. Washington, D.C.: National Library of Medicine, 1960– .
> Indexes the world's medical literature in about 3,000 periodicals. Issued monthly. Cumulates annually into *Cumulated Index Medicus.* Monthly issues and annual cumulations are divided into a subject section and an author section. A Bibliography of Medical Reviews appears in each monthly issue and cumulates annually. A list of periodicals indexed appears in the January issues and in the annual volumes.

Physical sciences

British Technology Index. London: British Library Association, 1962– .
Issued monthly with cumulations. A subject index of periodicals published in Great Britain mainly in the fields of engineering and chemical technology. Includes pure science where related to industries.

Chemical Titles. Washington, D.C.: American Chemical Society, 1961– .
Issued biweekly. Indexes over 600 journals in pure and applied chemistry. Each issue is in three parts: a keyword index of titles, a bibliographic listing of titles of current papers from selected journals arranged in the form of tables of contents of the journals, and an index of authors.

Index Chemicus. Philadelphia: Institute for Scientific Information, 1960– .
A twice-monthly indexing-abstracting service for literature on new chemical compounds and syntheses. Each issue contains author and molecular formula indexes which are cumulated four times a year.

Engineering Index. New York: Engineering Index, Inc., 1906– .
Covers mechanical, electrical, and civil engineering, and related subjects. International in scope. Indexes an extensive list of engineering and industrial periodicals, publications of scientific and technical societies, government bureaus, experiment stations, universities, and other research organizations, and conference and symposium papers. Includes brief abstracts. In a classified arrangement with author index. Issued annually with weekly card service prior to October, 1962. Issued monthly since October, 1962. Cumulates into the *Engineering Index Annual.*

4. Newspaper indexes

Newspaper indexes are similar in use to periodical indexes. Articles are listed by subject.

Some of the frequently used newspaper indexes are:

Christian Science Monitor Index. Boston: Christian Science Monitor, 1960– .
A subject index giving references to date, page, and column. Indexes Eastern, Midwestern, Western, and overseas editions. Monthly with six months and annual cumulations.

New York Times Index. New York: New York Times, 1851– .
A subject index giving references to date, page, and column, and cross references to names and related topics. Besides indexing the *New York Times*, it also serves as an independent index to dates and as a guide to other newspapers. Issued biweekly with annual cumulations.

Times, London. *Index to the Times.* London: Times Office, 1907– .
Detailed index referring to date, page, and column. Issued bimonthly. Titled *The Annual Index to the Times*, 1906–13; *The Official Index to the Times*, 1914–1957.

————. *Palmer's Index to the Times Newspaper, 1790–1905.* 65 vols. New York: Kraus
Reprint, 1965.
> Covers the *Times* almost from its beginning. Briefer information than in the
> *Official Index.*

Wall Street Journal Index. New York: Dow Jones & Company, 1958–   .
> In two sections: Corporate News and General News. Compiled from the final
> Eastern edition. Issued monthly with annual cumulations.

5. Abstract journals

Closely related to periodical indexes are abstract journals, which serve both to list
articles and books and to give summaries of their contents. There are abstract journals for
many subject areas. Below is a sample entry from *Historical Abstracts* with explanation.

```
ECONOMIC HISTORY
  10:3211 James, Francis G. (Tulane U.). IRISH COLONIAL TRADE
    IN THE EIGHTEENTH CENTURY; William and Mary Q. 1963 20 (4):
    574-584. Concludes that Irish exports to the colonies,
    though limited in scope, were of sizable proportions, and
    Irish imports from the American Colonies showed "a healthy
    if modest growth." The Irish trade benefitted the ports of
    New York and Philadelphia. Based on customs records.
    E. Oberholzer.
```

ECONOMIC HISTORY—Subject heading
10—volume number of Historical Abstracts
3211—number of the abstract
James, Francis G.—author
Tulane U.—location of author
IRISH COLONIAL TRADE . . . —title of article
William and Mary Q.—*William and Mary Quarterly* (title of periodical)
1963—date of publication
20 (4)—volume 20, issue 4
574–584—paging
Concludes that . . . —abstract
E. Oberholzer—abstractor

The following list includes abstracts of fairly broad coverage, representative of the
major subject areas.

Humanities

Abstracts of English Studies. Champaign, Ill.: National Council of Teachers of English,
1958–   .
> A monthly publication giving abstracts of articles in the field of English studies
> from American and English periodicals. Listed by titles of periodicals, with
> subject index.

American Literature Abstracts. San Jose, Calif.: Burbank Press, 1967– .
> Issued semiannually. Abstracts, written by the authors of the articles, are grouped in sections according to conventional divisions of American literary periods. Also includes a book review section.

Language and Language Behavior Abstracts. Ann Arbor: University of Michigan, Center for Research on Language and Language Behavior, 1967– .
> Issued quarterly. Covers more than 1,000 journals in over twenty languages. In a classified arrangement with author index.

America: History and Life: A Guide to Periodical Literature. Santa Barbara, Calif.: Clio Press, 1964– .
> An abstract journal including articles on American history from the earliest times to the present, on current American life, and on the history of Canada and current Canadian life. Surveys about 500 periodicals from the United States and Canada, some foreign periodicals, and certain types of books containing separate articles. Three issues per year. In a classified arrangement with annual subject and personal name indexes.

Historical Abstracts, 1775–1945. Santa Barbara, Calif.: Clio Press, 1955– .
> A quarterly journal of abstracts of articles on political, diplomatic, economic, social, cultural, and intellectual history for the period 1775–1945 in current periodical literature of all countries of the world.

Abstracts of New World Archaeology. Salt Lake City, Utah: Society for American Archaeology, 1959– .
> Issued annually. Includes all published titles dealing with New World archaeology and master's and doctoral theses. In a geographical arrangement with author index.

Philosophic Abstracts. 16 vols. New York: Philosophic Abstracts, 1939–1954.
> International in scope. All abstracts are in English.

Religious and Theological Abstracts. Youngstown, Ohio: Theological Publications, 1958– .
> Abstracts from Christian, Jewish, and Muslim journals in several languages. Issued quarterly with annual author, subject, and biblical indexes.

Social sciences

Child Development Abstracts and Bibliography. Chicago: University of Chicago Press, 1927– .
> Issued three times per year. Each issue includes abstracts of articles in a classified arrangement, a Book Notices section listing books by author with a brief review of each, and a list of books received. Author and subject indexes cumulate annually.

Economic Abstracts. The Hague: Martinus Nijhoff, 1953– .
> A semimonthly review of abstracts on economics, finance, trade and industry, management and labor. International coverage. Includes abstracts of books, periodical articles, and reports of governmental agencies and international organizations.

Geographical Abstracts. London: Department of Geography, London School of Economics, 1966– .

> In four parts: A. Geomorphology; B. Biogeography, Climatology, and Cartography; C. Economic Geography; D. Social Geography. *Geomorphological Abstracts* published separately 1960–1965. Abstracts of world literature in a classified arrangement. Issued six times per year with annual author and regional indexes.

International Political Science Abstracts. Oxford: Basil Blackwell, 1951– .

> Abstracts of articles of interest to political scientists appearing in leading professional journals of all countries. Major sections are: Political Science, Political Theory, Government and Public Administration, Government Process, International Relations, Area Studies. Issued quarterly.

Sociological Abstracts. New York: Sociological Abstracts, 1953– .

> Abstracts of books and articles, in a classified arrangement. International in scope. Eight issues per year including cumulated subject and author indexes.

Biological sciences

Biological Abstracts. Philadelphia: BioSciences Information Service of Biological Abstracts, 1926– .

> "A comprehensive abstracting and indexing journal of the world's literature in theoretical and applied biology, exclusive of clinical medicine." (Subtitle.) Issued biweekly with annual cumulative author, systematic, and subject indexes.

Excerpta Medica: The International Medical Abstracting Service. Amsterdam: Excerpta Medica, 1947– .

> Abstracts articles from medical journals published in many countries. Issued monthly in twenty-three sections. Each monthly issue includes subject and author indexes. Indexes cumulate annually.

Psychological Abstracts. Lancaster, Pa.: American Psychological Association, 1927– .

> Abstracts of the world's literature in psychology and related subjects. Includes articles, books, reports, and dissertations. In a classified arrangement. Issued monthly with an author index for each issue and annual author and subject indexes.

Physical sciences

Chemical Abstracts. Easton, Pa.: American Chemical Society, 1907– .

> The most comprehensive of the abstract journals covering the world's chemical literature in 9,000 journals. Issued semimonthly. Each issue has a numerical patent index, patent concordance, author index, and keyword index. Annual cumulations plus a formula index. Five-year cumulative indexes.

U.S. Geological Survey. *Abstracts of North American Geology*. Washington, D.C.: Government Printing Office, 1966– .

> Abstracts of technical papers and books, and citations of maps, on the geology of North America including Greenland, West Indies, Guam, and other island pos-

sessions of the United States. Issued monthly. Arranged alphabetically by author with a subject index. Abstract journals in the field of geology covering earlier periods are: *Geological Abstracts* (New York: Geological Society of America, 1953–1958), and *GeoScience Abstracts* (Washington, D.C.: American Geological Institute, 1959–1966).

Mathematical Reviews. Providence, R.I.: American Mathematical Society, 1940– .
A monthly abstract journal with international coverage of articles, books, research papers, and government publications in pure and applied mathematics and some aspects of physics. Monthly author index; semiannual author and subject indexes.

Meteorological and Geoastrophysical Abstracts. Boston: American Meteorological Society, 1950– .
Abstracts in English of current meteorological and geoastrophysical material published in several languages; bibliographical references to other items of interest to the profession; annotated bibliographies on subjects of special interest to meteorologists. Issued monthly.

Science Abstracts. Section A: *Physics Abstracts.* London: Institution of Electrical Engineers, 1898– .

Science Abstracts. Section B: *Electrical and Electronics Abstracts.* London: Institution of Electrical Engineers, 1898– .

Science Abstracts. Section C: *Computer and Control Abstracts.* London: Institution of Electrical Engineers, 1966– .
All three sections cover periodicals, books, dissertations, technical reports, and patents. International in scope. Section A is issued biweekly; Sections B and C, monthly. Comprehensive author and subject indexes published twice yearly for each section and cumulated for longer periods. The cumulated indexes also include cumulations of the bibliography, book, conference, patent, and report indexes from each issue of the abstract journals.

U.S. Atomic Energy Commission. *Nuclear Science Abstracts.* Washington, D.C.: Government Printing Office, 1948– .
A comprehensive abstracting and indexing coverage of international nuclear science literature. Issued semimonthly. Covers scientific and technical reports of the AEC and its contractors, other U.S. government agencies, other governments, universities, and industrial and research organizations. It also covers books, conference proceedings, conference papers, patents, and journal literature. Each issue includes four indexes: subject, personal author, corporate author, and report number. Indexes are cumulated semiannually and annually.

6. Government publications

Government publications should not be overlooked as a source of valuable material. Publications of federal, state, local, and international agencies cover a great variety of subjects. Such publications range from documentary material of historical interest to current developments in the scientific fields.

U.S. Superintendent of Documents. *Monthly Catalog of United States Government Publications*. Washington, D.C.: Government Printing Office, 1895–   .

> A current bibliography of publications issued by all branches of the government. Documents are listed by departments or bureaus with full title, date, paging, and price for each. Subject index.

United Nations. Library. Documents Index Unit. *United Nations Documents Index*. Lake Success, N.Y.: 1950–   .

> A monthly checklist of publications of the United Nations and specialized agencies. Each issue has a subject index which is cumulated annually.

Canada. Department of Public Printing and Stationery. *Canadian Government Publications: Monthly Catalog*. Ottawa: The Queen's Printer, 1953–   .

> Issued monthly. In two sections, English and French, each subdivided into parliamentary publications, departmental publications, periodicals, and index.

Great Britain. H. M. Stationery Office. *Government Publications: Catalogue*. London: H. M. Stationery Office, 1923–   .

> Issued monthly with annual cumulations. The monthly list is in three sections: parliamentary, nonparliamentary (departments and international organizations), and periodicals. Author, title, and subject index. The annual catalog is a cumulation of the monthly lists, with international organizations' publications listed in a supplement since 1955.

There are also lists of the publications of other national, international, state, and local agencies.

The *Public Affairs Information Service Bulletin* (see page 131) indexes many government publications by subject.

7. Pamphlets

Another source of information is pamphlets, valuable particularly for subjects of current interest. In addition to separately published titles, there are a number of pamphlet series such as those listed below.

Behind the Headlines. Toronto: Canadian Institute of International Affairs, 1955–   .

Headline Series. New York: Foreign Policy Association, 1935–   .

Public Affairs Pamphlets. New York: Public Affairs Committee, 1938–   .

The *Vertical File Index* (New York: H. W. Wilson Company, 1932–   ) is a monthly listing of pamphlets by subjects with an index of titles cumulated annually.

The *Public Affairs Information Service Bulletin* (see page 131) and the *Education Index* (see page 132) list pamphlets as well as periodical articles and other publications.

A reference librarian can be of assistance in locating pamphlet material in a library.

8. Dissertations

Graduate students may be interested in doctoral dissertations that have been written in their field of interest. The two sources below provide listings of dissertations by subjects and authors. It is possible to purchase copies of most doctoral dissertations from University Microfilms, Ann Arbor, Michigan.

American Doctoral Dissertations. Ann Arbor, Mich.: University Microfilms, 1957– .
> Annual listing of doctoral dissertations accepted by American universities. Arranged by subjects, and by universities under each subject. Author index. Titled *Index to American Doctoral Dissertations,* 1955/56–1962/63. Preceded by *Doctoral Dissertations Accepted by American Universities* (New York: H. W. Wilson Company, 1934–1955), and U.S. Library of Congress, *List of American Doctoral Dissertations Printed from 1912–1938* (Washington, D.C.: Government Printing Office, 1913–1940).

Dissertation Abstracts. Ann Arbor, Mich.: University Microfilms, 1952– .
> Abstracts of doctoral dissertations available in complete form on microfilm. Arranged by subject with author index. Issued monthly. Annual author and subject indexes. Beginning with vol. 27, no. 1, July, 1966, published in two sections: A. Humanities and Social Sciences; B. The Sciences and Engineering. Title changed to *Dissertation Abstracts International* in July, 1969, with the addition of dissertations from European universities. Preceded by *Microfilm Abstracts,* 1938–1951.

9. Archives and manuscripts

For some research projects it may be necessary to use original source material. This type of material must be consulted in the library where it is deposited. It is possible in some cases to obtain microfilm or photocopies for research use.

The two sources listed below are general guides to archival and manuscript collections.

Guide to Archives and Manuscripts in the United States. Edited by Philip M. Hamer. New Haven, Conn.: Yale University Press, 1961.
> A guide to the archival and manuscript holdings of more than 1,300 depositories in the United States, with summary descriptions of their holdings. Types of records described are business account books, diaries, sermons, church registers, war documents, personal correspondence, memoirs, municipal transactions, and legal records. Detailed index by subjects and personal names.

National Union Catalog of Manuscript Collections. Washington, D.C.: Library of Congress, 1962– .
> Lists manuscript collections housed permanently in American repositories regularly open to scholars. Six volumes, 1959–1967, describe more than 20,000 collections in 660 repositories. Issued annually since 1965. General index including subjects, places, personal names, and corporate bodies; and repository index.

10. Interlibrary loan service

Graduate students have the privilege of borrowing from other libraries through the interlibrary loan service of their own college or university libraries. If books, articles, or other materials found through bibliographies, indexes, and abstracts are not available in their own libraries, students may obtain them from the interlibrary loan service.

C. REFERENCE WORKS BY SUBJECT FIELDS

The following lists include encyclopedias, dictionaries, handbooks, histories, and biographical sources for the major subject fields. Tools for finding references on particular subjects—bibliographies, indexes, and abstract journals—are listed on pages 123–137.

Because of limited space, the following lists are brief and very selective. They are limited to works in the English language and to works of broad scope in each field. There are many other excellent reference works, some broad in scope and others devoted to specialized aspects of particular fields, which are valuable sources of information for students writing papers.

General

Encyclopedia Americana. International ed. 30 vols. New York: Americana Corporation, 1969.

Encyclopaedia Britannica. 24 vols. Chicago: Encyclopaedia Britannica, Inc., 1969.

Columbia Encyclopedia. Edited by William Bridgwater and Seymour Kurtz. 3d ed. New York: Columbia University Press, 1963.

Annual Register of World Events. London: Longmans, Green and Co., 1761–   .

World Almanac and Book of Facts. New York: Newspaper Enterprise Association, 1868–   . Annual.

New Century Cyclopedia of Names. Edited by Clarence L. Barnhart. 3 vols. New York: Appleton-Century-Crofts, 1954.

Chambers's Biographical Dictionary. Edited by J. O. Thorne. Rev. ed. New York: St. Martin's Press, 1968.

International Who's Who. London: Europa Publications, 1935–   . Annual.

Humanities

Art

Encyclopedia of World Art. 14 vols. New York: McGraw-Hill Book Company, 1959–1964.

Adeline, Jules. *Adeline Art Dictionary: Including Terms in Architecture, Heraldry, and Archaeology, with a Supplement of New Terms* by Hugo G. Beigel. New York: Frederick Ungar Publishing Company, 1966.

Upjohn, Everard M., Paul S. Wingert, and Jane G. Mahler. *History of World Art.* 2d ed. rev. and enl. New York: Oxford University Press, 1958.

Murray, Peter, and Linda Murray. *Dictionary of Art and Artists.* New York: Frederick A. Praeger, 1965.

Who's Who in Art. London: Art Trade Press, 1927–   . Biennial.

Dance

Chujoy, Anatole, and P. W. Manchester, eds. *Dance Encyclopedia.* Rev. and enl. ed. New York: Simon & Schuster, 1967.

Raffé, Walter G. *Dictionary of the Dance.* New York: A. S. Barnes and Company, 1964.

De Mille, Agnes. *Book of the Dance.* New York: Golden Press, 1963.

Sachs, Curt. *World History of the Dance.* Translated by Bessie Schönberg. New York: W. W. Norton and Company, 1937.

Drama

Gassner, John, and Edward Quinn. *Reader's Encyclopedia of World Drama.* New York: Thomas Y. Crowell Company, 1969.

Bowman, Walter P., and Robert H. Ball. *Theatre Language: A Dictionary of Terms in English of the Drama and Stage from Medieval to Modern Times.* New York: Theatre Arts Books, 1961.

Hartnoll, Phyllis, ed. *Oxford Companion to the Theatre.* 3d ed. London: Oxford University Press, 1967.

Sobel, Bernard, ed. *New Theatre Handbook and Digest of Plays.* 3d ed. New York: Crown Publishers, 1959.

Nicoll, Allardyce. *World Drama from Aeschylus to Anouilh.* New York: Harcourt, Brace & Co., 1950.

Rigdon, Walter, ed. *Biographical Encyclopaedia and Who's Who of the American Theatre.* New York: James H. Heineman, 1966.

History

Cambridge Ancient History. 12 vols., 5 vols. plates. Cambridge: Cambridge University Press, 1923–1939.

Cambridge Medieval History. 2d ed. 8 vols. Cambridge: Cambridge University Press, 1911–1936.

New Cambridge Modern History. Cambridge: Cambridge University Press, 1957–   . (In progress)

Langer, William L., ed. *Encyclopedia of World History: Ancient, Medieval, and Modern Chronologically Arranged.* 4th ed. rev. and enl. Boston: Houghton Mifflin Company, 1968.

Palmer, Alan W. *Dictionary of Modern History, 1789–1945.* London: Cresset Press, 1962.

Adams, James T., ed. *Dictionary of American History.* 2d ed. rev. 6 vols. and index. New York: Charles Scribner's Sons, 1942–1963.

Oxford Classical Dictionary. Oxford: Clarendon Press, 1950.

Dictionary of American Biography. Edited by Allen Johnson. 22 vols. New York: Charles Scribner's Sons, 1928–1958.

Dictionary of National Biography. Edited by Sir Leslie Stephen and Sir Sidney Lee. 22 vols. London: Oxford University Press, 1921–1922.

Literature

Cassell's Encyclopaedia of Literature. Edited by S. H. Steinberg. 2 vols. London: Cassell & Company, 1953.

Encyclopedia of World Literature in the 20th Century. Edited by Wolfgang B. Fleischmann. New York: Frederick Ungar Publishing Co., 1967–   . (In progress)

Columbia Dictionary of Modern European Literature. New York: Columbia University Press, 1947.

Thrall, William F., and Addison Hibbard. *Handbook to Literature.* Rev. and enl. by C. H. Holman. New York: Odyssey Press, 1960.

Hart, James D. *Oxford Companion to American Literature.* 4th ed. New York: Oxford University Press, 1965.

Harvey, Sir Paul, ed. *Oxford Companion to English Literature.* 4th ed. rev. by Dorothy Eagle. Oxford: Clarendon Press, 1967.

Harvey, Sir Paul, and J. E. Heseltine, eds. *Oxford Companion to French Literature.* Oxford: Clarendon Press, 1959.

Harvey, Sir Paul, ed. *Oxford Companion to Classical Literature.* Oxford: Clarendon Press, 1937.

Literary History of the United States. Edited by Robert E. Spiller and others. 3d ed. 2 vols. New York: Macmillan Company, 1963.

Oxford History of English Literature. Edited by Frank P. Wilson and Bonamy Dobrée. Oxford: Clarendon Press, 1945–   . (In progress)

Music

Grove's Dictionary of Music and Musicians. Edited by Eric Blom. 5th ed. 9 vols. London: Macmillan & Co., 1954.

————. *Supplementary Volume to the Fifth Edition.* Edited by Eric Blom. London: Macmillan & Co., 1966.

Thompson, Oscar. *International Cyclopedia of Music and Musicians.* Edited by Robert Sabin. 9th ed. New York: Dodd, Mead & Company, 1964.

Apel, Willi. *Harvard Dictionary of Music.* 2d ed. rev. and enl. Cambridge, Mass.: Belknap Press of Harvard University, 1969.

New Oxford History of Music. London: Oxford University Press, 1954–   . (In progress)

Baker's Biographical Dictionary of Musicians. 5th ed. compl. rev. by Nicolas Slonimsky. New York: G. Schirmer, 1958.

————. *1965 Supplement.* By Nicolas Slonimsky. New York: G. Schirmer, 1965.

Philosophy

Edwards, Paul, ed. *Encyclopedia of Philosophy.* 8 vols. New York: Macmillan Company and The Free Press, 1967.

Urmson, James O., ed. *Concise Encyclopedia of Western Philosophy and Philosophers.* New York: Hawthorn Books, 1960.

Wuellner, Bernard. *Dictionary of Scholastic Philosophy.* Milwaukee: Bruce Publishing Co., 1956.

Copleston, Frederick C. *History of Philosophy.* 8 vols. London: Burns, Oates & Washbourne, 1946–1966.

Kiernan, Thomas. *Who's Who in the History of Philosophy.* New York: Philosophical Library, 1965.

Religion

Encyclopedia of Religion and Ethics. Edited by James Hastings. 12 vols. New York: Charles Scribner's Sons, 1908–1927.

Schaff-Herzog Encyclopedia. *New Schaff-Herzog Encyclopedia of Religious Knowledge . . .* Edited by Samuel M. Jackson. 13 vols. Grand Rapids, Mich.: Baker Book House, 1951–1954.

Jewish Encyclopedia: A Descriptive Record of the History, Religion, Literature, and Customs of the Jewish People from the Earliest Times to the Present Day. 12 vols. New York: Funk & Wagnalls Company, 1901–1906.

Catholic Encyclopedia: An International Work of Reference on the Constitution, Doctrine, Discipline, and History of the Catholic Church. 16 vols. New York: Encyclopedia Press, 1907–1922.

Hastings, James, ed. *Dictionary of the Bible: Dealing with its Language, Literature and Contents Including the Biblical Theology.* 5 vols. New York: Charles Scribner's Sons, 1907–1909.

Mathews, Shailer, and Gerald B. Smith. *Dictionary of Religion and Ethics.* New York: Macmillan Company, 1921.

Smith, William, and Henry Wace, eds. *Dictionary of Christian Biography, Literature, Sects, and Doctrines.* 4 vols. London: John Murray, 1877.

Social sciences

General

International Encyclopedia of the Social Sciences. 17 vols. New York: Macmillan Company and The Free Press, 1968.

Worldmark Encyclopedia of the Nations. Edited by Moshe Y. Sachs. 3d ed. 5 vols. New York: Worldmark Press, 1967.

Gould, Julius, and William L. Kolb. *Dictionary of the Social Sciences.* New York: Free Press of Glencoe, 1964.

Zadrozny, John T. *Dictionary of Social Science.* Washington, D.C.: Public Affairs Press, 1959.

American Men of Science: A Biographical Directory. Vols. 7 and 8: *The Social and Behavioral Sciences.* 11th ed. New York: R. R. Bowker Company, 1968.

Anthropology

Anthropology Today: An Encyclopedic Inventory. Chicago: University of Chicago Press, 1953.

Winick, Charles. *Dictionary of Anthropology.* New York: Philosophical Library, 1956.

International Dictionary of Regional European Ethnology and Folklore. Copenhagen: Rosenkilde and Bagger, 1960– . (In progress)

People of All Nations: Their Life Today and the Story of Their Past . . . Edited by J. A. Hammerton. 7 vols. London: Educational Book Co., 1922–1924.

Penniman, Thomas K. *A Hundred Years of Anthropology.* 3d ed. London: Gerald Duckworth & Co., 1965.

Economics

Palgrave's Dictionary of Political Economy. Edited by Henry Higgs. 3 vols. London: Macmillan and Company, 1925–1926. Reprint ed. New York: Augustus M. Kelley, 1963.

McGraw-Hill Dictionary of Modern Economics: A Handbook of Terms and Organizations. New York: McGraw-Hill Book Company, 1965.

Seldon, Arthur, and F. G. Pennance, comps. *Everyman's Dictionary of Economics: An Alphabetical Exposition of Economic Concepts and Their Application.* London: J. M. Dent & Sons, 1965.

United Nations. Department of Economic and Social Affairs. *World Economic Survey.* New York: United Nations, 1947–   . Annual.

Cambridge Economic History of Europe from the Decline of the Roman Empire. Cambridge: University Press, 1941–   . (In progress)

World Who's Who in Commerce and Industry. 14th ed. Chicago: Marquis Who's Who, 1966.

Education

Monroe, Paul, ed. *Cyclopedia of Education.* 5 vols. New York: Macmillan Company, 1911–1913.

Encyclopedia of Educational Research. Edited by Robert L. Ebel. 4th ed. New York: Macmillan Company, 1969.

Good, Carter V. *Dictionary of Education.* 2d ed. New York: McGraw-Hill Book Company, 1959.

Foshay, Arthur W., ed. *Rand McNally Handbook of Education.* Chicago: Rand McNally & Company, 1963.

World Survey of Education. 4 vols. Paris: UNESCO, 1955–1966.

Meyer, Adolphe E. *Educational History of the Western World.* New York: McGraw-Hill Book Company, 1965.

Who's Who in American Education. Hattiesburg, Miss.: Who's Who in American Education, 1928–   . Biennial.

Geography

Larousse Encyclopedia of World Geography. New York: Odyssey Press, 1965.

McGraw-Hill Illustrated World Geography. New York: McGraw-Hill Book Company, 1960.

Columbia Lippincott Gazetteer of the World. Edited by Leon E. Seltzer. New York: Columbia University Press, 1962.

Stamp, Sir L. Dudley, ed. *Dictionary of Geography.* New York: John Wiley & Sons, 1966.

British Association for the Advancement of Science. Research Committee. *Glossary of Geographical Terms.* Edited by Sir L. Dudley Stamp. 2d ed. New York: John Wiley & Sons, 1966.

Dickinson, Robert E. *The Makers of Modern Geography.* London: Routledge & Kegan Paul, 1969.

Law

Lawyer's Encyclopedia. Englewood Cliffs, N.J.: Prentice-Hall, 1963.

Black, Henry C. *Black's Law Dictionary: Definitions of the Terms and Phrases of American and English Jurisprudence, Ancient and Modern.* 4th ed. St. Paul, Minn.: West Publishing Company, 1951.

Shumaker, Walter A., and George F. Longsdorf. *Cyclopedic Law Dictionary Defining Terms and Phrases of American Jurisprudence, of Ancient and Modern Common Law, International Law, Civil Law, the French and Spanish Law, and Other Juridical Systems, with an Exhaustive Collection of Legal Maxims.* Edited by Frank D. Moore. 3d ed. Chicago: Callaghan and Company, 1940.

American Jurisprudence: A Modern Comprehensive Text Statement of American Law, State and Federal. 2d ed. compl. rev. and rewritten . . . Rochester, N.Y.: Lawyers Cooperative Publishing Company; San Francisco: Bancroft-Whitney Co., 1962– . (In progress)

Cushman, Robert E. *Leading Constitutional Decisions.* 12th ed. New York: Appleton-Century-Crofts, 1963.

Political Science

Cyclopedia of American Government. Edited by Andrew C. McLaughlin and Albert B. Hart. 3 vols. New York: D. Appleton & Company, 1914. Reprint ed. New York: Peter Smith, 1949.

Mitchell, Edwin V. *Encyclopedia of American Politics.* New York: Greenwood Press, 1968.

Sperber, Hans, and Travis Trittschuh. *American Political Terms: An Historical Dictionary.* Detroit: Wayne State University Press, 1962.

Elliott, Florence, and Michael Summerskill. *Dictionary of Politics.* 5th ed. Baltimore: Penguin Books, 1966.

Political Handbook and Atlas of the World: Parliaments, Parties and Press . . . New York: Published for the Council on Foreign Relations by Harper & Row, 1927– . Annual.

Harmon, Mont J. *Political Thought: From Plato to the Present.* New York: McGraw-Hill Book Company, 1964.

Who's Who in American Politics: A Biographical Directory of United States Political Leaders. Edited by Paul A. Theis and Edmund L. Henshaw, Jr. 2d ed. New York: R. R. Bowker Company, 1969.

Sociology

Theodorson, George A., and Achilles G. Theodorson. *Modern Dictionary of Sociology.* New York: Thomas Y. Crowell Co., 1969.

Mitchell, G. Duncan, ed. *Dictionary of Sociology.* Chicago: Aldine Publishing Co., 1968.

Encyclopedia of Social Work. Edited by Harry L. Lurie. New York: National Association of Social Workers, 1965– .

Faris, Robert E. L. *Handbook of Modern Sociology.* Chicago: Rand McNally & Company, 1964.

Ogburn, William F., and Meyer F. Nimkoff. *A Handbook of Sociology.* 5th ed. rev. London: Routledge & Kegan Paul, 1964.

Barnes, Harry E., and Howard Becker. *Social Thought from Lore to Science.* 3d ed. 3 vols. New York: Dover Publications, 1961.

Science

General

McGraw-Hill Encyclopedia of Science and Technology. Rev. ed. 15 vols. New York: McGraw-Hill Book Company, 1966.

Van Nostrand's Scientific Encyclopedia. 4th ed. Princeton, N.J.: D. Van Nostrand Company, 1968.

Ballentyne, Denis W. G., and Louis E. Q. Walker. *Dictionary of Named Effects and Laws in Chemistry, Physics, and Mathematics.* 2d rev. and enl. ed. New York: Macmillan Company, 1961.

Graham, Elsie C., ed. *Basic Dictionary of Science.* New York: Macmillan Company, 1965.

Sarton, George. *Introduction to the History of Science.* 3 vols. Baltimore, Md · Published for Carnegie Institution by Williams and Wilkins Company, 1927–1948.

McGraw-Hill Modern Men of Science. New York: McGraw-Hill Book Company, 1966.

American Men of Science: A Biographical Directory. Vols. 1–6: *Physical and Biological Sciences.* New York: R. R. Bowker Company, 1965–1967.

———. *Supplements.* New York: R. R. Bowker Company, 1966– .

World Who's Who in Science: A Biographical Dictionary of Notable Scientists from Antiquity to the Present. Edited by Allen G. Debus. Chicago: Marquis-Who's Who, 1968.

Agriculture

Bailey, Liberty H. *Cyclopedia of American Agriculture: A Popular Survey of Agricultural Conditions, Practices, and Ideals in the United States and Canada.* 4 vols. New York: Macmillan Company, 1907–1909.

———. *Standard Cyclopedia of Horticulture.* 6 vols. New York: Macmillan Company, 1914–1917.

―――, and Ethel Z. Bailey. *Hortus Second: A Concise Dictionary of Gardening, General Horticulture and Cultivated Plants in North America*. New York: Macmillan Company, 1941.

Dictionary of Gardening: A Practical and Scientific Encyclopaedia of Horticulture. Edited by Fred J. Chittenden. 2d ed. by Patrick M. Synge. 4 vols. Oxford: Clarendon Press, 1956.

―――. *Supplement*. Edited by Patrick M. Synge. 2d ed. Oxford: Clarendon Press, 1969.

Winburne, John N., ed. *Dictionary of Agricultural and Allied Terminology*. East Lansing: Michigan State University Press, 1962.

U.S. Department of Agriculture. *Yearbook of Agriculture*. Washington, D.C.: Government Printing Office, 1894– . Annual.

Astronomy

Rudaux, Lucien, and G. de Vaucouleurs. *Larousse Encyclopedia of Astronomy*. 2d ed. New York: Prometheus Press, 1962.

Weigert, Arnold, and H. Zimmermann. *Concise Encyclopedia of Astronomy*. New York: American Elsevier Publishing Company, 1968.

Space Encyclopedia: A Guide to Astronomy and Space Research. New rev. ed. New York: E. P. Dutton & Company, 1960.

Wallenquist, Ake. *Dictionary of Astronomical Terms*. Edited and translated by Sune Engelbrektson. Garden City, N.Y.: Natural History Press, 1966.

Flammarion, Camille. *Flammarion Book of Astronomy*. New York: Simon & Schuster, 1964.

Shapley, Harlow, and Helen E. Howarth. *Source Book in Astronomy*. New York: McGraw-Hill Book Company, 1929.

Shapley, Harlow. *Source Book in Astronomy, 1900–1950*. Cambridge, Mass.: Harvard University Press, 1960.

Biology

Gray, Peter, ed. *Encyclopedia of the Biological Sciences*. 2d ed. New York: Van Nostrand Reinhold Company, 1970.

―――. *Dictionary of the Biological Sciences*. New York: Reinhold Publishing Corporation, 1967.

Henderson, Isabella F., and William D. Henderson. *Dictionary of Biological Terms: Pronunciation, Derivation, and Definition of Terms in Biology, Botany, Zoology, Anatomy, Cytology, Genetics, Embryology, Physiology*. 8th ed. by J. H. Kenneth. Princeton, N.J.: D. Van Nostrand Company, 1963.

Altman, Philip L., and Dorothy S. Dittmer, eds. *Biology Data Book*. Washington, D.C.: Federation of American Societies for Experimental Biology, 1964.

Sirks, Marius J., and Conway Zirkle. *Evolution of Biology*. New York: Ronald Press, 1964.

Chemistry

Encyclopedia of Chemistry. Edited by George L. Clark. 2d ed. New York: Reinhold Publishing Corporation, 1966.

Kingzett, Charles T. *Kingzett's Chemical Encyclopedia: A Digest of Chemistry and Its Industrial Application*. Edited by D. H. Hey. 9th ed. London: Ballière, Tindall & Cassell, 1966.

International Encyclopedia of Chemical Science. Princeton, N.J.: D. Van Nostrand Company, 1964.

Hackh's Chemical Dictionary: Containing the Words Generally Used in Chemistry, and Many of the Terms Used in the Related Sciences of Physics, Astrophysics, Mineralogy, Pharmacy, Agriculture, Biology, Medicine, Engineering, Etc. 4th ed. compl. rev. and ed. by Julius Grant. New York: McGraw-Hill Book Company, 1969.

Handbook of Chemistry and Physics: A Ready-Reference Book of Chemical and Physical Data. Edited by Robert C. Weast. 50th ed. Cleveland, Ohio: Chemical Rubber Co., 1969.

Partington, James R. *History of Chemistry*. New York: St. Martin's Press, 1961– . (In progress)

Farber, Eduard. *Great Chemists*. New York: Interscience Publications, 1961.

Engineering

Jones, Franklin D., and Paul B. Schubert. *Engineering Encyclopedia: A Condensed Encyclopedia and Mechanical Dictionary for Engineers, Mechanics, Technical Schools, Industrial Plants, and Public Libraries, Giving the Most Essential Facts About 4500 Important Engineering Subjects*. 3d ed. New York: Industrial Press, 1963.

Engineers Joint Council. *Thesaurus of Engineering Terms*. New York: Engineers Joint Council, 1964.

Perry, Robert H., ed. *Engineering Manual: A Practical Reference of Data and Methods in Architectural, Chemical, Civil, Electrical, Mechanical, and Nuclear Engineering*. 2d ed. New York: McGraw-Hill Book Company, 1967.

Souders, Mott. *Engineer's Companion: A Concise Handbook of Engineering Fundamentals*. New York: John Wiley & Sons, 1966.

Finch, James K. *Story of Engineering*. Garden City, N.Y.: Doubleday & Company, 1960.

Hart, Ivor B. *Great Engineers*. London: Methuen & Co., 1928. Reprint ed. Freeport, N.Y.: Books for Libraries Press, 1967.

Who's Who in Engineering: A Biographical Dictionary of the Engineering Profession. 9th ed. New York: Lewis Historical Publishing Co., 1964.

Geology

Fairbridge, Rhodes W., ed. *Encyclopedia of Earth Science Series.* New York: Reinhold Publishing Corporation, 1966–   . (In progress)

Bertin, Leon. *Larousse Encyclopedia of the Earth.* New York: Prometheus Press, 1961.

American Geological Institute. *Glossary of Geology and Related Sciences, with Supplement.* 2d ed. Washington, D.C.: American Geological Institute, 1960.

Mather, Kirtley F., and Shirley L. Mason. *Source Book in Geology.* New York: McGraw-Hill Book Company, 1939.

Mather, Kirtley F., ed. *Source Book in Geology, 1900–1950.* Cambridge, Mass.: Harvard University Press, 1967.

Adams, Frank D. *Birth and Development of the Geological Sciences.* New York: Dover Publications, 1954.

Geikie, Sir Archibald. *Founders of Geology.* 2d ed. London: Macmillan & Co., 1905. Reprinted. New York: Dover Publications, 1962.

Mathematics

Universal Encyclopedia of Mathematics. New York: Simon & Schuster, 1964.

International Dictionary of Applied Mathematics. Princeton, N.J.: D. Van Nostrand Company, 1960.

James, Glenn, and Robert C. James. *Mathematics Dictionary.* Multilingual ed. 3d ed. Princeton, N.J.: D. Van Nostrand Company, 1968.

Korn, Granino A., and Theresa M. Korn. *Mathematical Handbook for Scientists and Engineers: Definitions, Theorems, and Formulas for Reference and Review.* 2d ed. New York: McGraw-Hill Book Company, 1968.

Merritt, Frederick S. *Mathematics Manual: Methods and Principles of the Various Branches of Mathematics for Reference, Problem Solving, and Review.* New York. McGraw-Hill Book Company, 1962.

Bell, Eric T. *Development of Mathematics.* 2d ed. New York: McGraw-Hill Book Company, 1945.

Bell, Eric T. *Men of Mathematics.* 2 vols. Harmondsworth, Middlesex: Penguin Books, 1953.

Medicine

Stedman, Thomas L. *Stedman's Medical Dictionary: A Vocabulary of Medicine and Its Allied Sciences, with Pronunciations and Derivations*. 21st ed. Baltimore, Md.: Williams and Wilkins Company, 1966.

Taber, Clarence W. *Cyclopedic Medical Dictionary: A Digest of Medical Subjects: Medicine, Surgery, Nursing, Dietetics, Physical Therapy, Treatment, Drugs*. 10th ed. Philadelphia: F. A. Davis Company, 1965.

Bauer, William W. *Today's Health Guide: A Manual of Health Information and Guidance for the American Family*. Chicago: American Medical Association, 1965.

Garrison, Fielding H. *Introduction to the History of Medicine, with Medical Chronology, Suggestions for Study, and Bibliographic Data*. 4th ed. rev. and enl. Philadelphia: W. B. Saunders Company, 1929.

Bailey, Hamilton, and W. J. Bishop. *Notable Names in Medicine and Surgery*. 3d ed. London: H. K. Lewis, 1959.

American Men of Medicine. 3d ed. Farmingdale, N.Y.: Institute for Research in Biography, 1961.

Physics

Encyclopedic Dictionary of Physics: General, Nuclear, Solid State, Molecular, Chemical, Metal and Vacuum Physics, Astronomy, Geophysics, Biophysics, and Related Subjects. Edited by J. Thewlis. 9 vols. New York: Pergamon Press, 1961–1964.

———— *Supplementary Volumes*. New York: Pergamon Press, 1966– .

Besançon, Robert M., ed. *Encyclopedia of Physics*. New York: Reinhold Publishing Corporation, 1966.

International Dictionary of Physics and Electronics. Edited by Walter C. Michels. 2d ed. Princeton, N.J.: D. Van Nostrand Company, 1961.

Condon, Edward U., and Hugh Odishaw, eds. *Handbook of Physics*. 2d ed. New York: McGraw-Hill Book Company, 1967.

American Institute of Physics. *American Institute of Physics Handbook*. 2d ed. New York: McGraw-Hill Book Company, 1963.

Magie, William F. *Source Book in Physics*. Cambridge, Mass.: Harvard University Press, 1963.

Laue, Max T. von. *History of Physics*. Translated by Ralph Oesper. New York: Academic Press, 1950.

Psychology and Psychiatry

Encyclopedia of Mental Health. 6 vols. New York: Franklin Watts, 1963.

English, Horace B., and Ava C. English. *Comprehensive Dictionary of Psychological and Psychoanalytical Terms: A Guide to Usage.* New York: Longmans, Green and Co., 1958.

Hinsie, Leland E., and Robert J. Campbell. *Psychiatric Dictionary.* 3d ed. New York: Oxford University Press, 1960.

Wolman, Benjamin B. *Handbook of Clinical Psychology.* New York: McGraw-Hill Book Company, 1965.

American Handbook of Psychiatry. 3 vols. New York: Basic Books, 1959–1966.

Alexander, Franz G., and Sheldon T. Selesnick. *History of Psychiatry: An Evaluation of Psychiatric Thought and Practice from Prehistoric Times to the Present.* New York: Harper and Row Publishers, 1966.

Watson, Robert I. *Great Psychologists: From Aristotle to Freud.* Philadelphia: J. B. Lippincott Company, 1963.

D. OUTLINE

If the student is dealing with a subject with which he is unfamiliar, he will need to do some reading before preparing an outline. If, however, he knows in a general way what he wishes to write about, he may prepare an outline in rough form and then seek information about each of the points in it. The outline can be worked out in more detail as new ideas and information are discovered. By beginning with an outline and changing it as he progresses in his research, the student avoids the possibility of forgetting important sections, and keeps in mind the relationships involved in the paper.

A good outline not only indicates the scope of the paper, but also the relationships of the several sections. The arrangement of major headings with subheadings under them clarifies the organization of the paper. The titles of the sections should express the ideas to be conveyed, yet be brief.

An outline may be a topic outline in which each heading is a word or phrase, or a sentence outline in which each heading is a complete sentence. Topic headings and sentence headings should not be mixed in one outline. Headings should be gramatically parallel. If the topic style is used, each heading should be a noun, noun substitute, or a noun phrase. A sample topic outline is given on page 14; a sentence outline on pages 15–16.

E. NOTE-TAKING

From the very beginning of a research project, it is extremely important to keep notes. Notes should be made on cards or slips of paper of uniform size. Cards or slips can be more easily organized than information from a notebook. After a preliminary reading, the material should be reread and notes taken on important passages, ideas, or facts.

Note cards or slips should contain the following bibliographic information entered near the top.

For a book

a. Author's full name in inverted order
b. Complete title of the book
c. Editor, translator, illustrator, author of preface, if any
d. Series and number, if any
e. Volume number, if applicable

f. Edition, if other than the first

g. Facts of publication (place, publisher, date)

h. Page reference

The author's name and the title should be taken from the title page. If the date of publication does not appear on the title page, the copyright date from the verso (back) of the title page is used.

For a periodical

a. Author's full name in inverted order

b. Title of the article in quotation marks

c. Title of the periodical, underlined

d. Series, if any

e. Volume number

f. Date

g. Paging

Noting this information when the source of material is at hand will avoid the necessity of rechecking later for complete information for footnotes and entries in the bibliography.

At the upper right corner of the card may be placed a subject heading or a section number which will identify the material and fit into the outline of the paper. The note should be entered below the bibliographic information. A note may consist of a summary of the content of the material read, a direct quotation, a paraphrase, or a reference to statistics, tables, or illustrations. If a note is a quotation, the original must be copied *exactly*, including punctuation, capitalization, and misspelled words, if any.

Below is an example of a note card:

```
                                                              111
  Riessman, Frank.   The Culturally Deprived Child.
       New York:  Harper & Row, 1962.  P. 1.


       In 1950 approximately 1 child out of 10 in the 14
       largest cities of the U.S. was culturally deprived.
       By 1960 the figure was 1 in 3.  Increasing trend
       is due to migration to urban centers.  By 1970, the
       estimate is 1 deprived child for every 2 in schools
       in large cities.

  Footnote 14
```

FIGURE A–4. Note card.

As reading and research progress, note cards should be organized according to the part of the outline to which each applies. As the student writes the paper, he can use the notes in the order in which they are filed. Footnotes should be numbered in sequence and the same numbers should be recorded on the note cards. When the paper is finished, the note cards can be alphabetized by author to supply the entries for the bibliography.

Index